Praise for *Stop K*

"In this new book, Karen shares her common sense and practical guidance. Our firm appreciates the thought and expertise provided as our HR consultant, and I look forward to having Karen's advice in the form of a book to share with our employees and clients."

—**Debby Abel**, president, Abel Personnel

"Karen Young is both an award-winning human resources leader and a dedicated, approachable expert on the full range of human resource priorities. She understands and engages fully on both the compliance side of HR and the culture side of it as well, which is why clients gain such incredible benefit from the services delivered by Karen and her team at HR Resolutions."

—**W. Douglas Wendt**, senior partner, Wendt Partners

"We have worked with Karen and HR Resolutions to implement these systems and have found we have a more streamlined onboarding process with our new hires as well as an excellent, neutral, resource for our staff members who may have questions or concerns. We consider Karen a part or our senior management team when it comes to her expertise in all things HR."

—**Tony Darcangelo**, CFO, Credo Technology Solutions, Harrisburg, PA

"A well-written and organized book that should be on every HR manager's desk! It should definitely be considered as required reading for college-level HR classes."

—Nikki Wenrich, HR analyst,
Commonwealth of PA HR Service Center

"Our firm works with Karen Young on our human resource matters, and her guidance gives us peace of mind that we are on track to not only do what is best for our employees but to keep us in compliance with the regulators. Karen's new book does a great job of putting you on the path for that same peace of mind."

—Tom Moul, CFO and principal, Stambaugh Ness, PC

"Karen has hit the bulls-eye with *Stop Knocking on my Door*. It's the ultimate HR reference for every small business (or larger business that has a small HR department.) She's right when she says, 'HR isn't rocket science' but acknowledges what you don't know can hurt you. Don't be fooled by its easy-to-read-and-understand format. This book will be the first place I reach for HR advice going forward."

—Ira S. Wolfe, president, Success Performance Solutions

"I've been blessed to know Karen professionally and personally for over a decade. Her passion for all things HR is undeniable and contagious. She's always up for a great debate over best practice or strategy of an issue. She has a phenomenal depth of human resource and business knowledge. I'm honored and privileged to have her as a mentor, friend, and guide."

—Melissa Washington, PHR, director of human resources,
JPL Creative

Stop
Knocking
on my Door

KAREN A. YOUNG, SPHR,SHRM-SCP

Stop Knocking
on my Door

DRAMA FREE **HR** TO HELP GROW YOUR BUSINESS

Published by Advantage, Charleston, South Carolina.
Member of Advantage Media Group.

ADVANTAGE is a registered trademark and the Advantage colophon is a trademark of Advantage Media Group, Inc.

Printed in the United States of America.

ISBN: 978-1-59932-651-1
LCCN: 2015951288
Back Cover Photo: Nathaniel Corn, Rissa Miller, *balance photography*

This publication is designed to provide accurate and authoritative information in regard to the subject matter covered. It is sold with the understanding that the publisher is not engaged in rendering legal, accounting, or other professional services. If legal advice or other expert assistance is required, the services of a competent professional person should be sought.

 Advantage Media Group is proud to be a part of the Tree Neutral® program. Tree Neutral offsets the number of trees consumed in the production and printing of this book by taking proactive steps such as planting trees in direct proportion to the number of trees used to print books. To learn more about Tree Neutral, please visit www.treeneutral.com. To learn more about Advantage's commitment to being a responsible steward of the environment, please visit www.advantagefamily.com/green

Advantage Media Group is a publisher of business, self-improvement, and professional development books and online learning. We help entrepreneurs, business leaders, and professionals share their Stories, Passion, and Knowledge to help others Learn & Grow. Do you have a manuscript or book idea that you would like us to consider for publishing? Please visit advantagefamily.com or call 1.866.775.1696.

TABLE OF CONTENTS

PART 1: THE PROPER SETUP

PART 2: BRINGING PEOPLE ON BOARD

PART 3: RUNNING THE SHIP

PART 4: PARTING WAYS

 **FOREWORD**

I first met Karen in 1999 after moving to Pennsylvania to open new offices for my family's safety shoe business. At the time, our company had about thirty-five employees, and we operated shoemobiles from North Carolina through New York City with five stores and nine shoe trucks. By the early 2000s, our company was expanding service throughout the Northeast. At the same time, our longtime HR consultant, Bill Bearding, was retiring to Arizona. It was during that time that Karen began to assist us. Initially, our relationship started small with a few complicated projects over a two- to three-year period. Karen came through with thoughtful and professional results in each case.

Between 2005 and 2008, our company more than doubled in size. Karen knew before me that Saf-Gard needed more HR help. We needed experience and professionalism but only on a part-time basis. After a few conversations, we asked Karen to be our company's HR manager as a consultant. She has been exceptional from day one. Karen's grasp on the many regulations we must meet in each state has allowed me and our company to focus on the shoe business. We feel confident Karen is keeping us on the right track related to our HR programs. With about two hundred employees today, Karen has helped develop our hiring, training, and virtually every other HR program from the ground up. Today, Karen is one of my top advisors, and I know I can rely on her judgment nearly every time. Probably one of Karen's greatest strengths is her ability to tactfully push back when she disagrees on a matter. It takes backbone and tact to be a great advisor, and Karen has both. She professionally makes her points and keeps us moving in the right direction.

Karen fits our company culture because she doesn't side too much with either the employer or employee. She stays in the middle, which helps ensure everyone is treated correctly and fairly. For all of the reasons above, I think Karen would be a strong candidate as a part-time HR manager for any organization.

One of my favorite "Karen" stories relates to the "short-term disability plan" and AFLAC programs we've implemented at our company. For several years, Karen had recommended both, and I had not wanted to do them. I "reasoned" they were not necessary, and also in the past we had opted to continue paying the salary for long-term employee's pay when they were out of work. My thoughts quickly changed when a few of our newer employees suddenly ended up in the hospital without coverage. Once I finally recognized the need, Karen quickly implemented the program she'd suggested for a few years, and now we have a better company because of it. Despite this story and many others like it, Karen has never once said, "I told you so." She provides the advice, and we are free to follow it or not. Time has proven that following the advice is almost always the best course.

—**PATRICK KUBIS**, president, *Saf-Gard Safety Shoe Co., Inc.*

ACKNOWLEDGMENTS

So many people to thank…

- It may sound odd coming from an HR professional, but I must thank God for every one of my successes and all the blessings in my life.

- My parents, John and Mary Ellen Milliken, who raised me to believe I could do anything I set my mind to. I hope I've done them proud.

- My dad, specifically, for teaching me work ethic.

- Barry Young, the best husband ever, is an extraordinary man. He's my best friend; he grounds me, he spoils me terribly, and he believes in me.

- Phyllis Webber, Ron McKinley, and Jerry Hiler—three managers who saw something in me a long, long time ago.

- Glenn Ames, who made me go out and talk to people I didn't know about this funny little idea I had about a business.

- Ryan Keith, formerly with the Harrisburg Regional Chamber and Capital Region Economic Development Corporation and now with Forgotten Voices International (forgottenvoices.org), who said, "Wow, what a great idea!" all the way back in 2004.

- Anne Zerbe, who introduced me to my first "big" client and continues to believe in what my company has to offer. Anne also completed the book's Compliance Audit!

- My staff (past, present, and future), for following me and embracing our mission.

- My clients, without whom I couldn't follow my passion.

- Kate Kohler, for encouraging me to attend the Sandler Client Summit, where I met Adam Witty of Advantage Media.

- Hannah Kohl, my amazing editor, who held my hand, made me think critically about my profession, and reminded me that it would all be okay.

- The entire staff of Advantage Media—every one of them has believed in me and heard the author inside trying to get out!

 **INTRODUCTION**

Welcome to HR

A music major. That's actually how it all started. After one semester with too many practice rooms and not enough money at the end of it all, I switched majors to business. That's what you did if you couldn't cut it as a music major at Lebanon Valley College.

While sifting through the course catalog, looking for something to fill the one slot I had for a second semester elective, I stumbled across organizational psychology—the scientific study of human behavior in the workplace. How we discover our calling and why we're called is often a mystery. Maybe the fact that I was interested in the class description at all should have been an indication, but after a few short weeks in the class, I had found my profession!

Back then, HR was called *personnel*. Since personnel wasn't a major at the time, I double-majored in business and psychology, weaving together everything I learned about business with everything I found fascinating about the mind and human behavior.

As I neared graduation, I chose to survey over a hundred personnel leaders across the United States, asking what they believed was more important: continuing my education or getting practical experience. The results were overwhelming; I was told to get some real-world experience because the only way to break into personnel was to move into the department from within a company. So to get a job in my chosen field, I needed experience. To get experience, I needed a job in my chosen field.

Personnel people had to understand work and business. They had to know what it was like on the inside. After an internship in a personnel department, I was unable to break into the profession and took a job in the hospitality industry. Three years after graduating, I got my big break—working as an accounting temp, processing payrolls for a restaurant holding company. I was in.

Sometime in the mid-1980s, the name of the profession changed from "personnel" to "human resources," maybe because someone finally realized that no resource is more important than the people who work for you.

Like you, I fell into HR accidentally, but I *love* it. I've had to accept that not everyone loves human resource management, but I hope that my passion for the profession will help even the most reluctant, accidental HR manager find something to love in the field. In my experience, when the HR pieces are falling into place, a business starts to run like a well-oiled machine.

People always ask, "How do you deal with this 'HR stuff' every day?" I understand that a life of living, breathing, and dreaming about HR isn't for everyone. But in a small business, *someone* has to handle the human resource "stuff." More often than not, that someone has absolutely no interest in human resources and/or no specific training outside of a seminar or two. And yet, that person has accidentally become responsible for their company's human resource management.

HR isn't rocket science, but it can be confusing and frustrating; it can also be rewarding and fulfilling, and I've helped many other people turn the corner and learn to embrace what quality HR management can do for their company (and for their state of mind). It's important to remember that you're not alone and you can indeed accomplish your accidental HR duties while watching a company grow and implement best practices that streamline processes and reduce the company's risk, making it a safe and nourishing place to work.

As an HR specialist, I can walk into a company and know right away whether or not it has good HR management in place. Without it, the work environment often shows negligence or lack of thought in regard to safety. There are more workplace accidents and a significantly higher risk of discrimination cases, even when unintentional. Without a good HR plan in place, a company will have higher turnover, so money is constantly being spent on training and recruiting. This constant training and recruiting turns into a spiral, which leads to higher rates for the company's unemployment insurance as well.

There are strategies that will help you manage your HR responsibility *right now*. I'll teach you how to protect yourself against unnecessary risk and exposure so you can continue to focus on your other job responsibilities—like running the company, for example. I hope you'll find that best-practice HR is a useful tool, helping you to conduct business in a respectful, responsible, and nourishing work environment.

The great secret of quality HR management is that when your employees are happy and safe, you get an increase in productivity, an increase in your bottom line, and a reduction in incidents, disruptions, and turnover. People want to work in an efficient organization where they are respected, where they respect others, and where everyone does his or her job. And when you do need to find someone new to cover a vacant position, these best practices are what will lead you to a fantastic new hire.

When you feel the thrill of finding an excellent new employee and get to watch this person grow and succeed (and your company as well), I think that you might just find a little love in your heart for human resources after all. It's certainly my goal that you do.

PART 1

The Proper Setup

 **CHAPTER 1**

What You Don't Know Can Hurt You

If you have even one employee on your payroll, you may be subject to federal, state, and local employment laws. Do you know if you're in compliance with the law? If one of the many local, state, or federal agencies comes knocking on your door, do you know how to protect yourself? Is your paperwork in order? Do you even *have* paperwork? There are things you need to know *right now* to make sure you're in compliance with the law. You don't want to risk becoming embroiled in a lengthy court case that could have been prevented by having the proper practices and documentation in place.

Table 1 is a good reference chart for the typical federal regulations that apply to companies with various numbers of employees. As soon as you have one employee, whether he or she is full-time or part-time, there are ten federal employment laws that you're responsible for.

If you've grown large enough to hire an employee, you've grown large enough to need an HR manager. If your company's not large, that person is *you!*

TABLE 1. REGULATIONS BY HEADCOUNT

These are the federal regulations that employers may be responsible for when they reach the listed employee count. Although this chart is focused on federal regulations, don't forget to check what state regulations apply to employers with one or more employees.

EMPLOYEE COUNT	REGULATION/STATUTE	
1	Drug-Free Workplace Act	Equal Pay Act
	Employee Retirement Income Security Act (ERISA)	Fair Credit Reporting Act (FCR)
	Fair Labor Standards Act (FLSA)	Privacy Laws
	National Labor Relations Act (NLRA)	Occupational Safety and Health Administration (OSHA) regulations
	Uniformed Services Employment and Reemployment Rights Act (USERRA)	Affordable Care Act (ACA)
	Federal Unemployment Tax Act (FUTA)	Immigration Reform and Control Act (ICRA)
	Federal Workers Compensation Laws	
10	OSHA Record Keeping	
15	Americans with Disabilities Act as Amended (ADAAA)	Title VII
20	Age Discrimination in Employment Act (ADEA)	Consolidated Omnibus Budget Reconciliation Act (COBRA)

50	Affirmative Action Program	Family and Medical Leave Act (FMLA)
100	Worker Adjustment and Retraining Notification Act (WARN)	EEO-1 Report

As you add more employees to your workforce, you add more complexity to your HR management, more interpersonal issues, and more employment regulations. As an owner, the pressure increases as you accept the responsibility of providing for more and more people; the money they earn working for you is their livelihood, and it gives them the ability to support their families. The work they do for you can add meaning and purpose to their lives. In turn, you promise to adhere to the regulations that were put in place to protect them.

With the advent of the Affordable Care Act, there are now thirteen regulations a company is responsible for as soon as it puts even one person on the payroll. These regulations apply even if the company doesn't offer medical benefits. Adhering to these regulations truly does help to ensure a safe, productive, and drama-free workplace for your employees, so you'll want to follow them.

It helps to remember that these regulations weren't put in place to punish employers; they were put in place to *protect employees*. If you can make that switch in your brain, it will make following the regulations a whole lot easier. Even if a regulation seems arbitrary or arcane, each and every one has come about because, once upon a time, someone did something bad that hurt himself, herself, or someone else. In an attempt to prevent that injury or injustice from happening again, a protective regulation was created and accepted and is now enforced.

In my experience, the well-being and safety of employees is at the top of the list of importance for nearly every CEO or business owner. Employers are much more likely to wake up at night in a sweat, saying, "I have to make a payroll" than they are to wake up saying, "I have to make a profit." When you worry about payroll, you're showing that you care about the people who work for you and not just about increasing your profits. Learning about and following the necessary regulations is another way that you can demonstrate true care and consideration for your employees.

STATE REGULATIONS

Each state has its own set of rules and regulations. It's up to you to familiarize yourself with the regulations for the state or states where your company does business. Many professionals believe my home Commonwealth of Pennsylvania has some of the strictest regulations in the nation, so what goes for Pennsylvania is usually a good high-water mark for the rest of the states, with one exception: California. California is a human resource world unto itself, with so many employee regulations that I can't even give you the number. In fact, the Society for Human Resource Management and HR Certification Institute offers special certifications especially for California HR professionals.

With so many rules and regulations to keep track of, it's hard to know which to follow first: Does local trump federal? Does state come before local? Instead of wading through a swamp of guesswork, simply follow the strictest authority. While federal regulations apply to all of the states, you may also be subject to a stricter local or state regulation.

For example, if the city of San Francisco has a stricter definition of protected classes than the state of California (which already has a stricter definition of protected classes than the federal government), then employers in San Francisco need to follow the San Franciscan regulations first. Even if you make a mistake, the agencies are going to work with you (rather than against you) if you've made your best attempt at a good-faith effort to follow the law.

THE AGENCIES

In this section, I'll give you an overview of each regulatory agency, including who they are, what they do, why they might come knocking on your door, and what you can do to minimize your risk of being out of compliance. First, however, there are two things that can help reduce your exposure regardless of the agency you're dealing with.

1. Document everything. The phrase you hear in real estate is "location, location, location." In human resources, it's "document, document, document." You don't need to put a detailed note into the employee file every time you have a conversation about X, Y, or Z, but by keeping accurate, timely, and consistent notes and records, you're going to minimize your risk in any situation and make life a whole lot easier for everyone. You don't need to be fancy—notes can be easily stored on your calendar or in your work log, day planner, or Franklin Planner. Some people prefer to send themselves an e-mail. Even a simple note (for example, "Talked to Karen about overtime today.") becomes stored and date-stamped. Two years from now, when someone's looking for proof to back up a claim, you'll be able to say, "Oh, yes, Mr. Investigator,

here's my note. We had a conversation about this." Proper documentation is a game changer.

2. Making a good-faith effort and being honest will serve you well as you work with the various agencies, even if you make mistakes. For example, you can call the Occupational Safety and Health Administration (OSHA), enter a voluntary program with them, and, in turn, be protected from citations for two years. The agencies want to help you. I have an investigator with the Pennsylvania Department of Labor and Industry whom I'll call before taking action when I'm not sure of something regarding wages or hours. Time and again, he's told me that advice is free; it's the errors that are costly. So do yourself a favor and "measure twice, cut once."

1. OCCUPATIONAL SAFETY AND HEALTH ADMINISTRATION (OSHA)

www.osha.gov

OSHA's job is to ensure that every employee is guaranteed a safe work environment, and OSHA's goal is to help employers have safe workplaces. OSHA's job is *not* to shake you down! If you don't have a safe workplace environment, it's OSHA's job to help you correct it. The premise of the law is to protect employees, and that's why OSHA is there.

Every employer has to follow OSHA's General Duty Clause. You can go to OSHA's website and read the full document, but the basic premise of the General Duty Clause is that an employer has a responsibility to provide a workplace that is "free from recognized hazards" that could cause harm.[1] That means it's our *duty* as employers to send our employees home whole and healthy, the same way they came to us when they were hired or when they started the day's shift.

If an employee gets hurt on the job, you're responsible. I like to explain it this way: if someone gets hurt in my house, I'm responsible for taking care of him or her. It seems like a no-brainer, but, time and again, negligence, a lack of time, or poor planning creates a situation that results in injury.

WHY THEY MIGHT KNOCK ON YOUR DOOR

When OSHA visits, they will come for a few reasons. For now, let's look at the two most common: complaints and targeted industries (those with higher-than-normal hazards).

When OSHA receives an employee complaint, that complaint will remain anonymous. With small employers, oftentimes the complaint is difficult to keep truly anonymous. Imagine this scenario: You didn't train your workers to properly lock up the saw blade, and Kevin's finger got chopped off. He's sitting there with a bandage, you forgot to pay his surgical bill, and an OSHA official is standing there, clipboard in hand, asking you about it. You can safely bet that the complaint came from Kevin. But in larger companies, complaints are easier to keep anonymous, which encourages workers to reach out to OSHA if they've already reached out to you, but the safety hazard (or perceived safety hazard) remains.

Another reason OSHA might come to visit is that certain industries are more dangerous than others, and OSHA focuses on them with laser-like precision. For example, physicians' offices have a lot

---

1 United States Department of Labor. "Sec. 5 Duties." https://www.osha.gov/pls/oshaweb/owadisp.show_document?p_table=OSHACT&p_id=3359.

of "sharps" or needles. That's a specific hazard, and it makes sense for OSHA to target recognized businesses and industries that contain recognized hazards. If we step back and look at why they operate this way, it makes sense to target hazards rather than just blanket the entire world of industry and business with random spot-checks. That's unrealistic. It's easier (and more sensible) for OSHA to target hazards and focus on inspecting locations that likely contain those hazards.

Other industries with more hazards than average include trucking, transportation, and industries that use heavy machinery or dangerous items like meat cutters—anything that could easily hurt people, even by mistake.

It's your right to refuse OSHA entry, as your business is private property. But if you look at the big picture and take human nature into consideration, it's better to let them in so they can do their job rather than irritate them and make them suspicious. It is your right to turn them away; however, I don't recommend it. They'll just come back irritated and holding a warrant. Now, instead of just looking at the blocked fire exit, they'll look at *everything*.

It *is* acceptable to say, "I'm sorry, the person that you need to speak with isn't available right now." If your office manager is responsible for your record keeping and safety notes, it's perfectly acceptable to say, "Our office manager is not available right now. He'll be back tomorrow. Can we schedule a time for you to meet with him?" Most likely, they're going to agree to wait, depending on the severity of the complaint. They don't want to set you up to fail. OSHA's goal is simply to correct any problems and to ensure a safe workplace for employees, not to take you down.

MINIMIZING YOUR RISK AND EXPOSURE

There are safety hazards in *every* environment. It drives me insane when I walk past an unattended file cabinet with an open drawer. A number of things could occur: It could tip on you. You could walk into it. You could scrape your arm on the metal. It's a common hazard, yet it's so simple to close the file drawer and remove that hazard. Be aware of your environment, and help your employees do the same. Awareness is the key point of any safety program.

If your employees have a complaint, listen to what they have to say. For example, if they're constantly saying, "The back door sticks so badly—I always have to go out the side way," then go find out why, and fix the door. Be aware of your environment.

Housekeeping makes a difference, so tidy up! You can't walk into a box in the hallway *if there's no box in the hallway.*

Beyond the General Duty Clause, which activates when you have one or more employees, you have to maintain certain statistical records of accidents once you have ten or more employees. The OSHA 300 log needs to be maintained "live" throughout the year to record any workplace accidents that occur. Each year, between February and April, you have to post a summary of those accidents, even if there haven't been any. Generally, the summaries should be posted in a conspicuous location where employees will see them— perhaps in the same location as your required federal and state law postings. (We have no affiliation with them but highly recommend www.allinoneposters.com as the least expensive site for the purchase of the required posters.)

Once you have ten or more employees, some of the very first things OSHA is going to request are your current OSHA logs and the logs for the five prior years. If you have them at the ready, you're ahead of the game, so don't be lax with yourself on this point. Having that log up to date helps OSHA and protects you.

2. US DEPARTMENT OF LABOR (DOL)

www.dol.gov

The DOL is responsible for many of the regulations you will deal with, including the Fair Labor Standards Act (FLSA), child labor laws, and the Consolidated Omnibus Budget Reconciliation Act (COBRA).

What COBRA boils down to is continuing health care after certain qualifying events. You are responsible for COBRA if you have twenty or more employees *and* you offer health care. COBRA requires specific notices and deadlines, so pay close attention to the regulations, and consult a professional. Many states have enacted what's called "mini-COBRA" for businesses with fewer than twenty employees.

The DOL is also responsible for enforcement of the Uniformed Services Employment and Reemployment Rights Act (USERRA). USERRA provides protection for our uniformed service personnel when they're deployed and reemployment provisions for when they return.

If an employee (who is also a member of the uniformed services) is deployed, the employer has to let that person go on deployment. Upon returning, that employee has a specific number of days to go to the employer and say, "I want my job back." This is the one thing that is *not* the employer's responsibility to track. It is the uniformed service employee's responsibility to come back within the specified time frame, which is determined by the amount of miliary service. If the employee comes back within that time frame, you must give the job back to him or her with the same seniority, pay, status, and other benefits determined by seniority.

This measure serves as a protection for employees serving in the armed forces; however, small businesses must know about and prepare for this possibility because it can put a strain on them. For example, say that your employee is deployed for one year, and you've had to fill the position in the meantime. The "replacement" is now integrated into your business and relies on you, so it's going to be hard to let the "replacement" go. Ideally, you'll have a way to integrate him or her into another position because when uniformed services employees request their jobs back, you will generally need to reinstate them as though they were never gone.

Since USERRA was enacted, none of the employers I've worked with have had any challenge with reinstating the employees upon their return. These employers simply said, "Welcome home." In fact, I think I've probably only had one employee who had to actually request reinstatement.

The DOL also monitors workers' statuses as *exempt* or *nonexempt* employees. While the specifics of this topic are complicated and changing rapidly, the basic premise of exempt and nonexempt will stay the same.

Exempt employees are ineligible for overtime pay and are generally salaried workers. Nonexempt employees are entitled to earn overtime and are generally hourly workers. Under this classification system, an exempt person is paid the same for a sixty-hour workweek as he or she is for a thirty-hour workweek. A nonexempt person's weekly earnings change based on the hours that he or she has actually worked.

HR INSIDER TIP: OVERTIME

Overtime is generally based on a standard of forty-hour workweeks. If a nonexempt employee works more than that, he or she must be paid overtime of at least 1.5 times their regular wage. In most circumstances, employers are not required to count vacations, holidays, or sick days when calculating overtime. For the purposes of overtime, a workweek must be defined as a period of seven consecutive days. However, the employer could calculate the workweek from Monday through Sunday or Saturday through Friday, no matter what the pay cycle is. I think a lot of employers might make that mistake. You have to count every hour and be mindful. Check your state regulations to see how they compare to the federal definition. Don't forget to double-check your state's wage and hour laws.

Exemption status is based upon a job's duties, regardless of the job title. Weekly earnings are the first exemption test described in the Fair Labor Standards Act, but what it ultimately comes down to are the duties of the position and how much discretion and independent judgment in matters of significance goes with the job. Your definition of *independent judgment* probably isn't the same as the DOL's, so there are checklists out there that can help you determine if a position should be exempt or nonexempt. If you don't get the answer you want from the checklist, then you might need to modify the job description.

WHY THEY MIGHT KNOCK ON YOUR DOOR

Most commonly, the DOL knocks on your door because of a wage complaint. Perhaps you didn't pay overtime properly. You may have minors working for you and find the child labor law people on your doorstep (child labor also falls under the DOL's umbrella).

The DOL may show up because of an employee/contractor (contracted freelancer) misclassification. The DOL has hired additional investigators simply to look at misclassification issues, which are generally brought to light in one of two ways. One way is through unemployment claims. When an independent contractor files for unemployment after his or her job is done, the employer responds to the claim by stating that the person was an independent contractor, not an employee. However, through the unemployment process, it may be determined that the contracted worker should have been classified as an employee. The other main source of misclassification issues is when an independent contractor gets hurt on the job. As an independent contractor, he or she is not covered by your workers' compensation. However, the workers compensation process may result in a determination that the individual was actually an employee.

I always recommend that employers start with the IRS guidelines as an initial guide to determine if they are classifying their workers correctly. The IRS provides an excellent form that can help you make an informed determination—it's called Form SS-8. If you're still not sure after answering these questions, you can actually submit the form to the IRS for a formal determination.[2] Of course, as with most

2 IRS. "Determination of Worker Status for Purposes of Federal Employment Taxes and Income Tax Withholding." http://www.irs.gov/pub/irs-pdf/fss8.pdf

employment law questions, you should seek the advice of knowledgeable counsel, as federal and state wage and hour laws are complex and often depend on the specifics of very particular circumstances.

MINIMIZING YOUR RISK AND EXPOSURE

The DOL is there to protect the rights of the workers under your care. They simply want to make sure that people are being paid properly and aren't being overworked or taken advantage of. If you are being proactive and staying on top of things, you can ensure a great relationship with the DOL.

Document everything. This step is key to minimizing your risk with every agency. If you can back up what you're saying with proof, it's going to make life a whole lot easier for everyone.

Ensure that your employees and independent contractors (if any) are properly classified. If they're independent contractors, treat them as such. Ideally, they will have their own business and will perform services for other businesses, not just your company. In addition, you don't supply them with equipment, you don't set their hours, and you don't tell them what to do. If you want to direct the work they do, put them on your payroll. With contracted employees, I don't care how many hours they work. I pay the invoice for the services per the contract. You're paying them for the service, not for the time they're with you.

Follow the rules when you hire minors. The rules are very specific, so be mindful of them.

Listen to your employees. If an employee comes to you and says, "I think I should be making overtime," he or she has probably done some homework, and you should probably look at it a little bit more closely. Be thankful that he or she came to you instead of going to an outside agency.

Be consistent. "Yes" means yes, and "no" means no, period, to everyone, all the time. Don't set yourself up for a complaint by playing favorites or by letting certain employees get under your skin.

3. EQUAL EMPLOYMENT OPPORTUNITY COMMISSION (EEOC)

www.eeoc.gov

The EEOC is responsible for enforcement of Title VII of the Civil Rights Act of 1964, as amended, and other federal, anti-discrimination laws. It ensures that employers don't discriminate based on race, color, national origin, sex, religion, and several other protected classifications. The federal, anti-discrimination laws also prohibit retaliation against an individual who complains of unlawful discrimination or other protected activity. Recently, the EEOC also prohibited discrimination based on sexual orientation. The EEOC prohibits discrimination in hiring, firing, wages, and terms and conditions of employment.

As America becomes more diverse, it also becomes more confusing. Simply put, if something has no bearing on an individual's ability to do the job, then look past it (even if you don't understand it). How in the world would a long beard prohibit or prevent against someone answering customer service phone calls? It just wouldn't.

When it comes to adhering to EEOC's rules, there are a million what-ifs, but the real truth of the matter comes down to whether something *affects an employee's ability to do the job*. Does a religious headscarf prevent someone from serving a cupcake? No. Neither does a wheelchair. Neither does an individual's sexual orientation, skin color, or genetics.

Many people panic when faced with something that might look like discrimination because they're afraid they'll be sued. If you've kept good records of job-related reasons for your actions, though, then it's easy to be confident in defending your actions. It's not religious discrimination to let employees go because they can't work the mandated schedule for all employees in that job classification, even if that scheduling conflict is because they've decided to start attending religious services more regularly. Make decisions based upon the job-related needs of the business, *not* the circumstances of the individual.

It's wise to stop, think, and make sure that you're on the level, but don't let fear prevent you from taking care of your business.

WHY THEY MIGHT KNOCK ON YOUR DOOR

There are two different kinds of discrimination that the EEOC is looking for: *disparate treatment* and *disparate impact.* Disparate impact discriminates against a group of protected individuals. Disparate treatment discriminates against an individual. If it's proven that minorities can't score as well as white people on the test because of the way it's written, then the test has a disparate impact on minorities.

The EEOC also responds to complaints of *unlawful harassment.* Most people immediately think of sexual harassment, but unlawful harassment also applies to any protected classification. It can be confusing. For example, a headscarf may be protected, but a nose ring is likely not, because the two objects do not represent the same value in that person's life. The head covering is likely for religious reasons and is therefore protected, but nose rings don't typically fall into a protected class. You may also hear from the EEOC if you fail to accommodate employees so they can continue to perform the essential functions of their job due to illness or disability.

In diversity and harassment training, which is a great way to reduce the risk of litigation and foster a productive workplace, the key word is *respect*. I don't have to agree with my coworkers' religious beliefs, but I have a responsibility to respect that it's their right to believe what they want, just as I expect them to respect my faith. I don't have to understand, I don't have to agree with it, I don't have to accept it, and I don't have to follow it, but I do have to respect it.

MINIMIZING YOUR RISK AND EXPOSURE

As a leader, you set the tone for a respectful workplace by the way that you treat your employees and the way that they are expected to treat each other.

Train your employees. The best way to minimize exposure is to help your employees understand what protected, unlawful harassment or discrimination is. Implementing anti-harassment, discrimination, and retaliation policies and conducting anti-discrimination, harassment, and diversity training is a good start to reduce your risk of complaints. As strange as it may seem, bullying is probably not harassment. It is most likely unacceptable under the policies of the company and is probably a violation of work rules, but it doesn't necessarily cross the line into unlawful harassment if it is not based on the person's gender, religion, national origin, or other protected classification. Bullying needs to be connected to a protected class before it becomes an unlawful harassment.

Document, document, document. Follow your policies and procedures. Investigate promptly and thoroughly. If you have a discrimination complaint, you're going to want to be able to show that everything that happens in your business—hiring, firing, promotions, and disciplinary actions—happens based on merit and ability, not because of favoritism or prejudice.

3A. AMERICANS WITH DISABILITIES ACT AMENDMENTS ACT (ADA/ADAAA)

www.ada.gov

The Americans with Disabilities Act (ADA), as amended, protects individuals with known and perceived disabilities. The ADA Amendments Act of 2008 (ADAAA) greatly expanded the ADA's definition of *disability*.

Suppose that someone walks in on crutches to apply for a job, and I say to my HR coordinator, "I wonder what her problem is." I have potentially protected that person under the ADA/ADAAA because I have perceived her as having a disability.

That said, you shouldn't be afraid of the ADA. Employers fear that once employees tell them that they have disabilities, they'll never be able to fire them, even if they have performance issues. That's just not true. Disability or no disability, employers are allowed to expect a certain level of performance from their employees. The essential functions of the job must be completed, with or without accommodation.

As soon as someone says, "I have a disability," it's the responsibility of the employer to protect that employee (and the company) under the ADA/ADAAA. To do that, the employer and employee must enter into what's called the *interactive dialogue*. This is a process by which you lay out the expectations of the company, ask the employee what he or she is able to do and what accommodations he or she might need, and continue the dialogue regarding what is or is not a reasonable accommodation.

For example, if you have an outstanding receptionist who is starting to have difficulty hearing, you might first notice behaviors like calls being transferred to the wrong people and messages being mixed up. These are things that are uncharacteristic for someone who's been a fantastic employee for years. After speaking to her and identifying the problem—hearing loss, not a performance issue—you can start the interactive process so that both the employee and the employer identify ways to accommodate her so that she can continue to perform her job.

The solution may be to install a fifty-dollar adapter for the handset, which is a reasonable accommodation. But what if the adapter costs $5,000 and your entire phone system only cost $3,000? That may *not* be a reasonable accommodation. At that point, you need to explore other reasonable alternatives (which may include reassigning her to another job). Only after you explore all other reasonable options should you consider terminating this employee.

A leave of absence is often considered a reasonable accommodation, but that doesn't mean it has to be for six months. You need someone doing that job, but before you make decisions, have the conversation and document everything you do or attempt to do to make it right. Don't set a bright line and terminate everyone after a set period of time is over.

The interactive process also protects *you*, the employer. If an employee has come in and said, "I have a hearing problem, but if you get me a headset, I won't have any more issues," the issues may, in fact, continue. In that case, you are dealing with a performance issue, not a disability issue, and can address it as such.

MINIMIZING YOUR RISK AND EXPOSURE

Write thorough and accurate job descriptions. During hiring, you should always present the job description to the candidates and ask, "Are you able to perform the essential functions of the job with or without reasonable accommodation?" If they look at the job description and agree to it, take them at their word.

Offer reasonable accommodations, but don't guess at how you would or would not be able to perform the job in his or her shoes. If the candidate says, "I can't stand for eight hours, but I can do the job if I have a chair," then enter into a dialogue with them. You can agree to get them a chair or, if that's not possible, you can say, "There's no room for a chair in that area, so we can't provide a chair. Would a stool work?" You've attempted a valid offer of accommodation, and now it's up to the candidate to accept or decline.

You are not a doctor. While it's our responsibility to comply with the ADA/ADAAA as soon as we learn that an employee has a disability or we "perceive it," it's also important to keep in mind, in an effort to protect the company, to not just grant an employee's requests without consulting a medical professional. If somebody tells you that medically, he or she needs a different chair, then you want a medical professional to confirm that claim and give you guidance. The medical professional may tell you, "For this condition, you need a chair with task arms on it, but you don't need the $400 chair the employee is asking for." Again, you gain all of this knowledge through the interactive dialogue.

Don't be afraid to get a second opinion. If your employee comes to you with medical documentation that seems too good to be true, check it out. The employee may also be self-diagnosing an issue, so it's important to get a professional medical opinion.

In all of this, be proactive, and don't bend to fear or prejudice. And you may find that entering into that dialogue leads you to a wonderful employee that you may previously have overlooked, not realizing how well they could perform the job.

4. US IMMIGRATION AND CUSTOMS ENFORCEMENT (ICE)

Formerly the US Immigration and Naturalization Services (INS)

www.ice.gov

US Immigration and Customs Enforcement (ICE) falls under the Department of Homeland Security, whose primary mission is to promote homeland security and public safety. ICE focuses on "smart immigration enforcement."

ICE has been directly involved with all employers since its creation in 2003. An employer's interaction with ICE has to do with an individual's eligibility to work in the United States. It has nothing to do with their citizenship or their culture. We document proof of employment eligibility through the I-9 form.

Employers should always be sure they are using the most current I-9 form, so double-check the expiration date on the form. On the I-9, there's a section for the employee to complete and a section for the employer. The area that employees most often miss is the actual "attestation" section, where they indicate their class of eligibility to work in the United States (for example, American citizen, permanent resident, or authorized alien).

You should absolutely *not* ask if someone is an American citizen during a job interview. Instead, you should ask, "Are you eligible to work in the United States?" That is a perfectly acceptable question. You do not need to be an American citizen to be eligible to work in the United States.

Similarly, you may *not* tell job candidates what items they should present for identification. Instead of asking for their driver's license and Social Security card, provide candidates with the list of acceptable documents listed on the I-9. You *may* say, "Most people present their driver's license and Social Security card." (It's semantics, I know, but...)

In my experience as a consultant, the I-9 is the largest record-keeping failure people make, simply because employers don't fill out the form correctly. Filling out the I-9 improperly can cost an employer anywhere from $110 to $16,000 in civil fines and can involve criminal penalties ranging from a $3,000 fine to six months in jail.[3] However, mistakes on the I-9 are usually simple to avoid. The instructions for filling out the form are on the form itself.

The most common mistake made by employers filling out the I-9 Employer Certification Section is forgetting to include the hire date. About 90 percent of people leave that line blank. It's in the small print right above the employer signature section. To fill it out correctly, enter the date on which the employee started working; otherwise, it's a line-item fine.

---

3 US Citizenship and Immigration Services. "Penalties." Last modified November 23, 2011. http://www.uscis.gov/i-9-central/penalties

WHY THEY MIGHT COME KNOCK ON YOUR DOOR

An ICE audit is more of a record-keeping audit, and ICE is the only agency required to give notice before an audit. If I were an agent doing an investigation into hiring illegal immigrants, I'd show up unannounced at your business or farm. But if I wanted to audit your documentation, I would schedule an appointment. Other agencies might come in and say, "I want to see a *sampling* of your record keeping. I want to see personnel files for five current employees and two terminated employees." ICE is different because they come in and say, "I want to see *all* your I-9s." They want everything.

In the days before your appointment, if you realize you've missed something on an I-9, you can and should correct it.

MINIMIZING YOUR RISK AND EXPOSURE

In addition to documenting everything, which is standard risk prevention for dealing with every agency, there are a number of things you can do to protect yourself.

Correct your mistakes. There's nothing wrong with you auditing your I-9s. I encourage you to do it, if needed, but to make sure you maintain a list of the errors that you discovered and the steps you took to correct those errors. *Document, document, document.* If ICE does come in, you can say, "We self-audited and found these errors. This is what we did to fix them." They'll appreciate the good-faith effort to correct any mistakes, but they'll definitely expect you to have kept records of any changes.

When making corrections, never, ever use whiteout on an I-9 or any other legal document. If you need to make a correction, use a single strike-through, and then date and initial the change.

If you decide that the whole I-9 form needs to be redone, do not destroy the original. Have the employee fill out a new form, and then attach the old form to the back of the new one so that you can demonstrate that the original document was filled out in the first seventy-two hours of employment, even if it was done improperly. Let them know that your audit revealed so many mistakes that your correction was to fill out a new form.

If you fail to fill out the form in the first seventy-two hours, don't try to back date. Similarly, don't back date new forms or corrections. Be honest. Make a true *good-faith effort*—that's the key phrase with all of the agencies. If you're demonstrating a good-faith effort, they will not want to punish you.

Ask for help. It's perfectly reasonable to call and ask for help or clarification. Our office calls E-Verify—a federal government database used to confirm information on the I-9—regularly. Federal contractors and some state contractors are required to use E-Verify.

Get familiar with filling out these simple forms. Make sure you're filling out every single line. This isn't something to gloss over or to pass off to an intern. This is serious business.

5. THE NATIONAL LABOR RELATIONS BOARD (NLRB) AND THE NATIONAL LABOR RELATIONS ACT (NRLA)

www.nlrb.gov

A common misperception is that the National Labor Relations Board (NLRB) deals only with union companies. That is a false assumption. The National Labor Relations Act (NLRA) covers nearly all employers, both union and nonunion.

The NLRA protects an employee's right to concerted activity. That means that employees are allowed to discuss wages, terms, and conditions of employment with anyone at any time. If your employee handbook says, "You may not discuss your wages with any other employee," then you are violating the NLRA.

Social media brought the NLRA to everyone's attention. An employee was fired after posting nasty stuff about his employer on social media. Seems logical, right? The problem is that some of his coworkers chimed in to the conversation, both agreeing and disagreeing. The minute coworkers entered that conversation, it became a protected, concerted activity. If none of his coworkers had chimed in, his termination may have been able to stand.

If someone is using social media to bash the company or complain about supervisors or coworkers, you can sit them down and ask, "Do you think that was really the best way to address your problem?" But do not ask the employee to take down the post or discipline that person for posting without determining whether the activity is protected. What employees do on their own time is generally their business, even if it's complaining about work. After your talk, hopefully the employee will take it upon himself or herself to take down the post and stop using social media as an outlet for work complaints.

The NLRA also addresses union elections and recognition of unions. While union membership is declining, this is a hot-topic agency, and it probably always will be. The unions have a really, *really* large voice in Washington.

I've worked in both union and union-free environments, and there are advantages and disadvantages to both. I wholeheartedly believe there's less of a need today for union representation than ever before. In my experience, unions will promise the world, but the realities of economics are such that a company can only provide what the company can provide. If I can't afford to provide 100 percent company-paid medical coverage, then I can't afford it, no matter what the union demands. And if I'm forced to offer something I can't afford, my only recourse may be to start laying people off or to close the business.

While you may not worry about an organizing campaign, you still need to be aware of this law, because the same rules apply: employees are allowed to congregate, they are allowed to discuss their wages, and they are allowed to discuss their work environment. And when they come to you, you're allowed to try to make things better, if you can.

WHY THEY MIGHT COME KNOCK ON YOUR DOOR

If you've violated your employees' right to congregate or their right to put up information about a union meeting in the break room, chances are you'll be hearing from the NLRB. If your social media policy is too restrictive and/or you discipline employees for their activities on social media, you'll most likely hear from the NLRB.

MINIMIZING YOUR RISK AND EXPOSURE

The best way to minimize your exposure is to make sure that you have a solid no-solicitation policy. But there's a compromise with that because "no solicitation" means *no solicitation*. So that means that you can't sell your daughter's Girl Scout cookies, just like the union can't pamphlet your workplace. Once you break your own rule, it's a free-for-all.

Since it's nearly impossible to enforce a strict "nothing" policy, it's best to compromise. Let your employees sell the Girl Scout cookies in non-work areas like the break room during non-work time, but know that it opens the door for an employee to put up union information in the same area. Whether you approve or not, it's better to know what's coming in the front door than to force everyone to sneak through the back door.

6. DEPARTMENT OF TRANSPORTATION (DOT)

www.dot.gov

If your business has any vehicles with a gross value weight (GVW) in excess of 10,000 pounds, they fall under certain Department of Transportation (DOT) regulations. At 26,000 pounds, a special license is required. For reference, a 10,000-pound vehicle could be something like a moving truck, and a 26,000-pound vehicle would be closer to a semi-truck. However, you need to consider every vehicle your business has—tractors, pickups, and so on.

Even if you only have vehicles under 10,000 pounds, you may still need to pay attention to DOT regulations. The setup that's most often overlooked is a pickup truck hauling a trailer with a piece of equipment on it. People tend to think of that setup as consisting of three separate entities, but as soon as they're linked together and/or stacked, they need to be counted as one vehicle for weight purposes. For example, you may have a setup where the pickup truck's GVW is 6,000 pounds, the tractor's GVW is 3,000 pounds, and the piece of equipment on the trailer's GVW is 2,000 pounds. You are now over 10,000 pounds, and there are certain record-keeping requirements for the commercial motor vehicle operator (that is your driver).

WHY THEY MIGHT KNOCK ON YOUR DOOR

If you don't have a DOT number or a number assigned by your local public utility commission, you're probably going to stay under the radar unless your driver is pulled over or involved in a crash. But a crash is the most common reason that DOT comes to your door. They may also become aware of your company through a roadside inspection, either at the weigh stations you pass on the highway or if your driver is pulled over for a traffic offense.

MINIMIZING YOUR RISK AND EXPOSURE

Know what equipment you have. Find out how much it weighs (it's generally posted right inside the door of the vehicle). Make a list of the ways you combine equipment, and find out how much those configurations weigh. Determine if your drivers need special licenses.

The very first level of record keeping is a medical certification card for the driver, a copy of his or her driver's license, and their driving record in the form of a motor vehicles report (MVR).

If you suspect that DOT requirements might pertain to you but aren't sure, give them a call. They are there to help you, to protect your employees, and to assist you in following standards.

With all agencies, remember that a good-faith effort goes a long way. If you're trying and you're open and honest with them, they'll work with you as you learn the various ins and outs of their requirements and regulations.

 **CHAPTER 2**

Job Descriptions

Job descriptions are at the hub of the wheel of successful human resource management. Everything else that you deal with comes out of job descriptions and works in concert to form a functioning unit. Lose one or two spokes, and you can hobble along. Lose the hub, and you're in the ditch.

You can recruit all you want, but your recruiting won't be successful unless you know exactly what you're looking for. Going forward, unless new employees understand exactly what their responsibilities are, they won't have successful onboarding/orientation periods. Without solid job descriptions, your coaching and mentoring lose their focus—you may advocate one thing one day and another thing the next. No one can be successful in an environment like that, and if you intend to discipline an employee for poor job performance, both of you need to have a deep understanding of what the job's expectations really are. And if someone is leaving their position (even when retiring or being promoted) or you have to terminate an individual, you want to fully understand what the job's responsibilities are and what will be required to fulfill them.

The best way to create a job description is by determining the *essential functions* of a job. Essential functions are a lot more than just the tasks of the job; they are the basic reasons why the job exists. To capture them, a job description should be written much like a résumé. For example, instead of saying, "Push the first button on the phone to answer an incoming call many times a day," you should say, "Answer heavy call loads." You don't need to get into the nitty-gritty of the actual process of the job, but you do want to describe the overall idea of the task or responsibility.

The Americans with Disabilities Act impacts job descriptions because when we talk about the interactive dialogue, we need to know what a job's *essential functions* are. We also need to know what physical and work-environment exposures are involved.

To illustrate essential functions, let's go back to our example of a receptionist. The essential functions of the job—the primary reasons the job exists—are to greet guests when they come in and to answer incoming calls. There might be other secondary responsibilities or tasks that the person does—the receptionist might match accounts payables to purchase orders or answer the phone—but the *purpose* of that job is to greet visitors when they come in and answer incoming calls. It's that simple.

Now let's look at how a job description might interact with the ADA and accommodations. The essential function of the job of *forklift driver* is driving the forklift. A secondary responsibility may include refilling propane tanks and putting them on shelves in the garage. Maybe an applicant can drive a forklift, but he can't lift heavy gas cans. Technically, he is still a good candidate because he can fulfill the essential functions of the position. Someone else can lift the gas cans.

HR INSIDER TIP: KEY POINTS TO WRITING A GOOD JOB DESCRIPTION

When writing a job description, here's a quick list of what to include:

- Job title
- The supervisor's title
- Essential function or functions of the job
- Secondary responsibilities
- Knowledge, skills, abilities, and qualifications required for the position
- The physical and work environment

When there's a small staff, everyone has to wear a lot of hats, so you can't necessarily capture everything in a single job description. Instead, outline the basic purpose for the job and include one or two sentences about why the position exists. Don't go overboard by including nonessential functions. Simply add, "All other duties, as assigned." That covers the rest and prevents employees from being able to use the old chestnut, "That's not in my job description."

An added feature that you can include in a job description is what's called *scope*—the depth and breadth of the position, such as how many people report to the position and the sales volume the position is responsible for. Describe some of the quantitative aspects of the job. This helps you in hiring and allows applicants to make their own determination about whether or not they're a good fit.

Another critical piece of information for the ADA is the *physical and work environment*. If the position requires sitting at a desk for an extended period of time while utilizing a computer and telephone, a health-care provider can read into that and determine that the employee would need to be able to sit for long periods of time and that the employee will be using their arms, fingers, and forearms.

Again, the physical and work environment characteristics need to be clear in the job description to avoid complications in the event that we need to enter into an interactive dialogue. Having these characteristics in place makes a difference, even in cases where you're dealing with workers' compensation and return-to-work programs. It's much easier to get an individual back to work if you can present the evaluating physician with a solid job description that covers the responsibilities of the position and the work environment. It's also better for the doctor to hear the responsibilities of the job from you and not from an injured employee, who may want extra time off work or who wants to come back before her or she is ready, risking another injury.

I also highly recommend including knowledge, skills, abilities, and qualifications (KSAQs) in a job description. This is where you talk about the soft skills necessary for the job—the characteristics, traits, knowledge, and/or education that support an individual's ability to be successful in the job—such as excellent time management skills or in-depth understanding of a computer programming language. These are the building blocks that employees bring with them, ready to put to use.

If possible, involve your employees in developing the job descriptions. Not only will they take more ownership of it, but no one knows the job better than the employee doing it. Working with your employees to develop the job descriptions will also reveal the additional tasks they've assigned themselves. For example, your accounts manager may be the one who covers breaks for the receptionist, but if your accounts manager leaves, someone else will have to take over the task.

No matter what tasks your employees take on or assign to themselves, you still have the final say. You can allow them to continue or tell them to cease and desist with a certain activity, such as lifting the fifty-pound tank onto the water cooler. When employees are a part of job description development, they'll have a better understanding of how they fit into and contribute to the overall success of the company.

BENEFITS OF A GREAT JOB DESCRIPTION

When a company has fantastic job descriptions, some really good things happen. First, your employees are crystal clear on their responsibilities and the responsibilities of their coworkers and supervisors. It brings a great deal of clarity to interpersonal work relationships, defining where one job stops, where another begins, and how they are all interconnected. It gives employees boundaries; they may offer to help another coworker with his or her task, but they are no longer obligated or pressured to do so.

If you have an injured worker or an employee that comes to you and says he or she has a disability, great job descriptions put you ahead of the game. You can't be accused of creating something after the fact because you can honestly say, "We've had these descriptions in place for six months now."

Great job descriptions also make it simpler to do performance evaluations. Instead of wasting time thinking about what should be evaluated, it's all right in front of you. Job descriptions can also help you uncover redundancies and duplicated efforts between departments.

One of my clients did an exercise where the company's employees had to come up with their own job descriptions. The CEO and the COO looked over them, everybody contributed input, and they got to what they felt were the final drafts. From there, my responsibility was to take the essential functions from each individual job and put them into a big matrix. In doing that, we improved efficiency by moving some tasks out of one person's job and into another person's job, where it made more sense.

It's not unusual to discover that the development person is covering some marketing responsibilities (even though there was a communications person on staff) or that the accountant is doing a little light HR. Look at your data, and reassign tasks to the appropriate departments so that your employees can get back to doing what they were hired for and what they're best at doing.

WHEN JOB DESCRIPTIONS ARE NONEXISTENT

You may not realize that you need a job description until one of your employees gets hurt at work and you have to talk to their doctor, until someone is threatening to call the DOL, or until the infighting amongst your employees over who's supposed to do what has reached a fever pitch.

If there's a workers' compensation issue and you have to make up a job description on the spot, you can be accused of crafting it to suit your immediate needs. The doctor is then put into the position of deciding who to believe—the employee, who's been doing the job for six months, or the employer, who just created the document.

One of the hidden challenges for CEOs is that it's tough for us to have job descriptions for ourselves, because we do so many jobs inside the company. For example, I'm in business development, which requires one set of skills. I am also the HR strategist, which relies on another set of skills. There are simply so many essential functions included in being a CEO that they almost go beyond definition. Perhaps the best job description for a CEO is, "Don't let the business fail and don't let anybody get hurt." That covers most of the bases.

If you've already hired everyone and you're just coming to the realization that you need to clarify the job descriptions, it's not too late. Carve a little time out of a staff meeting and say, "We're going to talk about job descriptions and how we affect each other." A discussion like that builds relevance and gets the ball rolling. People are more committed to their organization if they understand how they fit into their departments and into the overall organization. It's not just about getting the tasks done but *how* the tasks are getting done and how they interrelate.

With a little forethought and diligence, you'll find that the work you put into defining job descriptions now will pay off time and again in the months and years to come.

 **CHAPTER 3**

Handbooks

Handbooks are the written document of your company's culture. They are the best piece of internal advertising that you have for your company. Not only do they promote internal branding, they help drive your mission, vision, and values.

Handbooks also reflect your company's personal tone and attitude. Are you a more formal organization? If so, your handbook is going to be written with more formal language. Is your company a more laid-back, hip, cool place? Use more lingo and relaxed language.

There is a school of thought out there that says, "You shouldn't have a handbook, because then you're stuck with the rules." This may be so, but your handbook is so much more than your rulebook. It should be your playbook, your guidebook: full of your expectations and goals as well as what your employees can expect of *you*.

It's a way to state to your employees that you are going to provide them with a safe workplace and fair and equitable salaries, wages, or benefits. It's also a way to tell them what you expect of them: to do their jobs well, to respect their coworkers, to treat the customers like family, and to restrict personal calls to breaks and lunches.

In addition, the ideal handbook should be relevant, meaningful, and user friendly. If you hand an employee a one-hundred-page employee handbook and tell them to read it that night and sign it, they're going to wait till you're gone, flip to the last page, and sign it; it becomes meaningless. You need to keep it meaningful—something they can read and refer to when they have basic questions about policy.

Some policies are fifteen to twenty pages of single-spaced information. That level of detail doesn't need to be in the handbook. Instead of including your whole drug-free workplace policy, simply state, "We are a drug-free employer and, as such, we follow an in-depth policy. For additional information and specifics on the policy, please see the drug-free workplace policy manual." In most cases, it's enough to let them know you have it (and where to find it).

HR INSIDER TIP: HOW LONG IS TOO LONG?

When it comes to handbook length, short and sweet is best. Some handbooks become more of a procedure manual than a true handbook. The two are not the same. Get your message across as succinctly as possible. If certain sections are getting long, it's probably a sign that a separate procedure manual is needed for that step.

TO HANDBOOK OR NOT TO HANDBOOK...

It's completely up to you whether or not you have a company handbook, but consider this: it's better to *not* have a handbook than to have a handbook you don't enforce. Enforcing the rules *sometimes* (or enforcing some policies but not others) will bite you in the rear every single time.

Say I terminate an employee for a clear violation of our policy against theft from coworkers. The evidence is clear: I've seen them take food and trinkets off of desks, and the whole thing is on video, so I terminate them. At the unemployment hearing, I win, but the former employee chooses to appeal. At the appeal hearing, the investigator asks, "Do you have an employee handbook? Do you have a policy against theft in the workplace? Did the employee sign the acknowledgment?" It looks like things are going great until the employee who took the food pipes up and says, "They also have an attendance policy. I've been late for work every week for a year, and I never got in trouble for that. How do I know which rules are real?" Because of your inconsistencies, the employee will likely get away with petty theft *and* get unemployment. If you're not going to enforce something, then take it out of the handbook.

I'd rather walk into an unemployment hearing and say that I don't have a theft policy but that it's common sense that stealing is wrong. The investigator will likely agree, and chances are the employee will not be getting unemployment this time around.

Because you should enforce and expect everything set forth in your handbook, you shouldn't offer something to employees that you aren't required to offer. One thing I see companies offering when they don't have to is family medical leave, which is governed by the Family Medical Leave Act (FMLA).

If a company has fewer than fifty employees, it is not required to offer family medical leave under the FMLA. That doesn't mean the company can't offer something similar. If the company believes in and has the ability to provide twelve weeks off for an employee under circumstances similar to the FMLA requirements, then by all means, it should have a similar policy.

CIRCUMSTANCES FOR WHICH FAMILY MEDICAL LEAVE MAY BE REQUIRED

- To care for a newborn child so long as leave is completed before the child's first birthday;
- Placement of a child for adoption or foster care so long as leave is completed before the one-year anniversary of the initial placement;
- To care for a spouse, child, or parent of an employee who requires such care because of a serious health condition;
- Because the employee has a serious health condition that renders him or her unable to perform his or her job;
- To care for an immediate family member of the Armed Forces, including a member of the National Guard or Reserves, who is undergoing medical treatment, recuperation, or therapy, is otherwise in outpatient status, or is otherwise on the temporary disability retired list for a serious injury or illness (may provide for more than 12 weeks); or

- Any qualifying exigency (as the Secretary of Labor shall, by regulation, determine) arising out of the fact that the spouse, son, daughter, or parent of the employee is on active duty (or has been notified of an impending call or order to active duty) in the Armed Forces in support of a contingency operation.

The challenge with offering FMLA coverage when it's not required is that as soon as you do, it's written in stone. Further, if you manage it incorrectly, you're going to be held to the same standards as a company that *is* required to offer it.

If you have challenges with an employee, you can use the handbook to help guide you through a conversation. You could say, "You know what, Jim, I'm noticing that we are having more and more discussions about policy violations and lack of respect for your coworkers. Let's have a conversation about why that's happening."

In meetings with frustrated employees, walk through the handbook and revisit the expectations to see if anything throws up a red flag. Help the employees pinpoint why they're upset. They may hate wearing a suit and tie every day or may strain against a typical nine-to-five schedule. Using the handbook as a tool, you can show them that a dress code and a fixed start time are there in black and white. Let them know that you're not going to change. If they're not okay with that, offer some suggestions for places that might be a better fit and come up with an exit strategy.

A WORD ON PROCEDURES

Your handbook is basically a policy that represents your expectations. Procedures are *behind* your expectations. For example, say that there is a company policy of random drug testing. This policy is outlined in the handbook, but the handbook doesn't need to contain the procedure of how participants are randomly selected, where they're going to go, how they're going to give their sample, or what's going to happen when the sample comes back. But I *have* a procedure, especially with something like drug testing, because I want to be sure that I am doing everything perfectly and consistently every time.

You can also have procedures behind your job descriptions. For example, if an employee is responsible for answering a heavy volume of calls, you might create a procedure that details how we go about answering a high volume of calls.

Procedures are much more likely to change than policies, especially when it comes with technological updates. It's important to note that if your procedures are woven through your handbooks, you'll have to reissue updates or the whole thing every time something changes.

In building a handbook, remember to cover the basics, include any required notices or policies, such as FMLA, keep it short, keep it simple, promote company culture, celebrate your perks, and make it something meaningful that employees will not only read but also refer to when they want to make sure they're in alignment with the rules.

 **CHAPTER 4**

Record Keeping

You will constantly hear me singing the praises of good record keeping. It's the best way to protect yourself, to prepare for employee meetings and evaluations, and to be at the ready should an agency or lawyer ever knock on your door.

In the "good ole' days" of personnel departments, everything went into one personnel file. Files would be inches thick, and we never got rid of anything—who knew when you might need to know what deductions Johnny had authorized in 1964. (If we did get rid of anything, it went right in the trash can; there were no shredders in those days—less identity theft way back then, too.)

Later, the Immigration Reform and Control Act of 1986 was enacted to reduce the employment of illegal aliens. The I-9 Form provided a list of various types of acceptable documents—specifically, documentation that may indicate an employee's national origin and race (protected classes). To the best of my recollection, that was when we began separating personnel documents into different areas. Next came the Americans with Disabilities Act of 1990 (ADA), which required employers to keep medical records confidential, and the Health Insurance Portability and Accountability Act of 1996 (HIPAA.) With HIPAA came the new phrase *protected health information*, reinforcing creation of a second file for medical records.

This file was to include any and all information about an employee's (including dependents) medical and health information, including benefit enrollment forms.

A few important things to remember:

- You have a duty to protect your employees' personal information, paying particular attention to Social Security numbers and personal health information.

- Access to personnel files should be on a need-to-know basis.

- Files should be kept secure with limited accessibility; medical files should be maintained in a confidential, separate file area with even less accessibility.

- I-9s should be kept separate from personnel and medical files, but they may be kept in a single, company-wide file.

- Old information should be shredded, not thrown away, especially if it contains any information that could identify the employee it is associated with.

When in doubt, err on the side of caution. Ask yourself if you would want the particular document or piece of information revealed about you personally, and treat it with that same respect.

SAMPLE PERSONNEL FILE CHECKLIST

The "traditional" file

- Employment application and résumé
- Reference checks
- College transcripts
- Job descriptions
- Records relating to the job: hiring, promotion, demotion, transfer, layoff, rates of pay, as well as other forms of compensation, and education and training records
- Records relating to employment practices
- Letters of recognition
- Disciplinary notices or documents
- Performance evaluations
- Test documents used in an employment decision
- Exit interviews
- Termination records

The "medical" file

- Medical/insurance records
- Physical/drug screen results
- Doctor's notes
- JFMLA certification requests/ approvals

The "someplace else" file

- I-9 form
- Safety training records
- Child support/garnishments
- Litigation documents
- Worker's compensation claims
- Requests for employment/payroll verification

If you have commercial motor vehicle operators, you need a driver qualification (DQ) file. This should have copies of all appropriate certifications and licenses for driving heavy machinery and/or large motor vehicles, background checks, annual MVRs, and the driver medical certification card. You should keep the DQ file separate from your other files (but equally confidential).

It's not uncommon to need additional records, such as training certifications, child abuse clearances, drug testing, clearance documents, and fingerprinting. Just make sure that you know whether each document regards general employment or is protected. If it's protected, it should be in the confidential file.

Many companies are converting (or have completely converted) to electronic files. If that is the case for your company, make sure that those electronic files are as secure as a locked safe, with protections, access codes, and safety assurances. To be honest, with all of the hacking that takes place in today's world, a good, old, locked filing cabinet often provides the most secure—and affordable—protection.

The benefit to keeping files on hand in paper form is that they are easy to whip out and share when the appropriate agencies come calling. With electronic files, you can always print out what's needed, but you need to remember that once confidential files are out of the computer, they must still be protected properly.

Ensuring your employees' right to privacy is your responsibility, and it's one you should take seriously.

PART 2

Bringing People
On Board

CHAPTER 5

Recruiting

Finding the right person for the job is critical, not just because you need to fill a position but because bringing in someone new can affect your office culture (and office culture affects how much drama comes knocking on your door). But if you do things right, you can end up with a great new hire who helps your company be successful for years to come. Do things wrong and, well …

People often look at recruiting as selection. I prefer to see recruiting as *sourcing to find the right person.* Instead of focusing on finding a miracle candidate, you want to focus on the very real possibility of finding lots of good candidates to consider.

Unlike job descriptions, where the main focus is to know what you're looking for, recruiting is all about finding a lot of candidates who can do what you need them to. To accomplish this, you need to know the hard skills (for the actual tasks) that the person will require, and you need to consider the soft skills (the characteristics or traits) that will ensure his or her success in your organization.

Using our example of a receptionist, the hard skill needed might be "able to answer phone calls," but there's more to it than that. Do you want someone who can answer the phone pleasantly and have a conversation with the caller? Or do you prefer someone who's a bit more direct? If you have a lot of incoming calls, you'll want the receptionist to find out where each call needs to go and move the calls along quickly. That takes certain soft skills, like being direct and focused on efficiency. Chattier individuals would be terribly uncomfortable in an environment where they need to move calls through like cows in a cattle chute. Their soft skills might be an ability to make everyone feel like an old friend or to calm nerves. Both have value; it just depends on what you want and what your company needs.

Soft skills are just as important as hard skills—maybe more so. We can train hard skills—typing, tightening bolts on a piece of machinery, transferring data—but it's much more difficult to train someone to answer the phone pleasantly.

Each position actually has two different sets of soft skills: corporate soft skills (characteristics that everyone in the organization must be able to demonstrate) and job-specific soft skills, which apply to that particular position only. Everyone at HR Resolutions must be able to work as part of a team (corporate soft skills). Our HR coordinator also needs to be very detail-oriented, while our project manager needs to have broad thinking skills with the ability to see the big picture (job-specific soft skills). Once you start thinking of your employees as a team, it's time to get a playbook.

When recruiting, many CEOs feel like they know the positions they're hiring for, inside and out. But let's go back to why we *document, document, document.* I want you to be able to protect yourself in three weeks from the person that you *don't* hire. If there's an issue or accusation, you want to be able to refer to your documentation and say, "This is what we were looking for before we even met you or started looking to fill the position. Based on our interview, you did not demonstrate the traits or characteristics needed to be successful in the position."

Like a playbook helps a team win a football game, determining what you need now and putting it down on paper will help you write your recruitment ad, determine the questions you're going to ask during screenings and interviews, evaluate how the candidates have done in the interviews, and, ultimately, make your selection. You're setting yourself up for success and making the hiring process easier.

Setting things down in stone also helps prevent you from hiring people for jobs they're not suited for just because you really like their personalities. (If someone came in who also adopted retired racing greyhounds, I'd naturally think they were perfect for whatever job needed doing!) It's human nature to identify with someone when you have a connection, but loving retired greyhounds isn't going to get the payroll done on time.

TIME, BUDGET, AND LOCATION

If you want to optimize your recruiting process, there are three things to think about: time, budget, and location.

As you plan your recruiting strategy, you need to consider how much time you have to find someone. The shorter time frame you have in which to find someone, the wider you should cast your net from the beginning. Did your operations manager give you a one-month notice? Is this a newly created position? Do I have a little time to shop around, or is this a critical fill? If the search is for my vice president of operations and I don't get someone in that position pronto, then I'm going to have to do *that* job along with *my* job, which adds a bit more urgency to the situation.

To keep yourself from overspending during the search, you need a recruiting budget. Know how much money you have and how you want to spend it. Just remember—you get what you pay for! I've had some great successes with craigslist.org, but that tends to run hot and cold because the right person has to be looking on the right day. A website like www.indeed.com, which has both free and paid options, draws a more work-focused crowd. The big paid online sites, such as www.monster.com and www.careerbuilder.com, draw from all over the world and have advanced algorithms working behind the scenes.

As you scout locations for your job ads, keep in mind that you are looking to find the passive job-seeker—the individual that's basically happy in their current job but is curious about what else is out there. Those people tend to go to the bigger, better-known sites, because they assume that way is quicker and faster (and it often is); but in some towns, it's still the local Sunday paper that gets all the hits.

Let's look more deeply into the importance of choosing where to advertise. If you're hiring for a warehouse person, you don't need to be doing a national search. The likelihood of someone moving across the country for a warehouse job is fairly low. But if you're looking for the dean of a college, a national search makes sense.

Where you advertise depends upon the position (and position level) in question. Bring in as many options as possible! The more specific the job and the higher up the ladder you go, the wider you'll have to cast your net. Lots of people can work as a cashier; fewer can blow a perfect piece of glass for a museum-quality vase or manage a national sales team in three languages.

> **The newspaper:** You can spend more on a newspaper ad than you could for a thirty-day or sixty-day job posting on paid websites, but in certain towns and for certain

types of jobs, people still use the newspaper as their go-to source.

Trade associations: If you're a publisher, utilize your publishing associations. If you're a trucking company, utilize American Trucking Associations. Trade associations are a fantastic resource and are usually a cost-effective way to advertise.

Industry job boards: Most industries have trade sites that include job boards. For example, in the theater industry, there are websites like www.playbill.com that cater to people who are passionate about theater and list jobs related to the industry. The same goes for nonprofits dealing with the arts, health, animal welfare, or any number of other categories. If you're looking for an office manager, why not find one who also happens to be passionate about your industry or cause?

Chamber of Commerce: The Chamber of Commerce works to connect businesspeople and is focused on business success and growth. The Rotary Club or other business associations also fall into this category.

Unemployment office: This is the source that nearly everyone forgets about, and they shouldn't. The unemployment office is a fantastic resource that is often underutilized because people tend to think of it as a place that draws from the bottom of the barrel. That is completely untrue. Outside of starting my own company, the best job I ever got came through my local unemployment office. Better still, recruiting through the unemployment office is free! You should post every single job opening you ever have with them.

When considering location, you should also think about populations of people that you may be overlooking. Thinking outside the standard corporate box can lead you to some truly exceptional candidates.

Veterans: Don't forget your veterans. They have had incredible training and know how to work as part of a team. In my town, we have Fort Indiantown Gap, which is associated with the Pennsylvania National Guard, but nearly every town in America has a veterans' organization or a VA office.

Seniors: AARP isn't necessarily a euphemism for *old people*. You can join AARP when you're fifty or older. Older employees often have a wealth of experience and understanding that can be a welcome resource in any business.

People with disabilities or physical challenges: You absolutely should not discount the disabled population in your area. *Disabled* does not mean crippled or unable to work. It means that someone is working with a physical challenge and may need accommodations. I think that sometimes, people overlook this part of the population because they're not sure how to incorporate an individual with physical challenges into their work environment. But there's a simple solution to that: contact any of your local nonprofit agencies that deal with individuals with disabilities and challenges. They will gladly help you determine which positions might be a good match. The Job Accommodation Network (JAN) is also a great resource.

People in transition and people returning to the workforce: As a country, I think Americans are still of a mind-set that when you make a job change, you should make more money. That's not the case anymore. Don't discount someone just because they're stepping out of management and want to go back into customer service. First, they know enough of what they want that they've left a good position to start over. Second, there is value in having people who are knowledgeable about a number of positions and fields. Similarly, don't discount someone who is returning to the workforce after taking time away.

It's important to remember that people who look the shiniest on the page aren't always the brightest when you take them out of the box. Go back to the essential function of the position. Who is best qualified to do the job? Let the essential functions lead you to the right person.

WRITING THE RECRUITMENT AD

Let's start with brass tacks: Never put the entire job description in the ad. I don't care how much room you have—an ad is not a job description; it's an opportunity to advertise your company.

Use the recruitment ad to talk about the great things that your company offers and what it can do for an individual. Attract potential candidates so they say, "I want to find out more!" Then, put in your minimum qualifications—a combination of hard and soft skills. Don't put too much in, or you might scare people off if they don't match bullet point number nineteen.

You should also use your recruitment ad as your first line of screening. If a bachelor's degree is needed to be successful in the position, that should be in the ad.

THIS IS A REAL AD ON CRAIGSLIST... *THIS IS BAD*

CDL DRIVER QUALIFICATION FILE SPECIALIST

I need someone experienced with creating and maintaining CDL Driver Qualification files. (DQ files)

We hire hundreds of CDL drivers per year, so you must be independent and knowledgable.

Please email your resume and salary requirements.

HERE IS A BETTER VERSION

CDL DRIVER QUALIFICATION FILE SPECIALIST

Seeking a team member who can work independently and is up-to-date on DQ requirements. Opportunity to create and develop our systems to stay compliant in a constantly changing environment. Please respond with your current resume and salary history.

NOTE THE DIFFERENCES:

- Knowledgeable—FYI...spelling counts in ads.

- Use the lingo—if they have experience, they'll know the lingo.

- Be positive.

- Don't assume they are going to send a current résumé—require it.

- Salary history is more important than salary requirements.

TRACKING RESPONSES

I like to track everything. I want to know who has responded from what source so that I can evaluate whether or not a source is working for me. I want to see my return on investment, even from a free ad. Am I getting qualified candidates from my craigslist ads? (Because if I'm getting sufficient candidates from a free ad, to heck with the paid ads the next time!) If you don't track it, you'll never know.

I do my tracking and my screening on a very simple Excel spreadsheet where I list the individuals and what source they came from. I list my minimum requirements across the top and then build in columns for hard skills, soft skills, salary history, and anecdotal notes.

As my responses come in, I record everything—who they are, where they come from, and if they meet the minimum qualifications. The more boxes a candidate checks, the higher the likelihood that I'm going to invite him or her in for an interview. In a situation where I'm accused of discriminating during hiring, I can present that document and say, "This individual was not considered because we hired based on these factors, and they did not do as well as such-and-such other candidate. It had nothing to do with their age, color, national origin, sex, religion, or genetic information."

As you proceed, you can add to that tracked data with the date of the interview and your interview ranking. That way, it's all right there in a single document. You can make a chart in your notebook, in Excel, or as a Word file. The key is to keep track of all your interviews in one place; it doesn't matter how you do it.

Creating an interview ranking is much like screening your responses. You actually conduct your interview and evaluate that interview immediately after you've done it, before you see anyone else. You want to make sure that the candidate meets the expectations and that you're interviewing for the things you're actually looking for.

These points reinforce why you should select one candidate and not another. It helps you on two levels—one, in choosing the best person for the job and not the one who you are most drawn to on a personal level; and two, to streamline the process and gather valuable data, should you ever need to defend your decisions.

HR INSIDER TIP: TYPOS ON RÉSUMÉS

There's an insider's reason for tossing résumés that are full of mistakes: If I run an ad and I get three hundred responses for one customer service position, I need to reduce that number of responses that I need to view. Or, if the ability to write word-perfect documents is one of the soft skills I'm looking for, the résumé already gives me an idea of whether they're qualified. You don't need to be a perfect speller to be an excellent candidate for other positions, though, so think about what you're looking for before you toss a résumé in the trash. You should be keeping the résumés for a couple months anyway, in case there's an issue.

As part of the screening process, be sure to ask for salary history. I strongly recommend asking for salary *history* instead of salary *requirements*. Here's why: Say I want to make a million dollars. I've never earned a million dollars at a company before, but that's what I feel I deserve. That's what I *require*. While my salary requirement is a million dollars, my needs more closely match what I made previously, as represented by my salary history. My last job paid $45k; that's a big discrepancy. Remember: a salary history can be fact-checked; salary requirements are based on needs, which are subjective.

PHONE SCREENING

Phone screenings helps you fill in details and get additional information before deciding whether or not to continue to the next level of the hiring process. They take up a lot less time than face-to-face interviews and require less commitment on the parts of both the employer and the potential employee. It's a good way for both of you to decide if you'd like to move forward.

If a candidate's response came in and met three out of four of your desired criteria, you can move that person to the next step in the process, which is a phone screening. During the screening, you should have three or four questions that will help you gain more information about the candidate. Again, you'll evaluate how he or she did on those questions based upon the essential functions and requirements of the position before determining if the candidate will move on to the next step: interviewing.

The thing to remember in all of this is that by spending a little time now, you are saving yourself huge amounts of time later, all while driving yourself toward the best candidate available.

 **CHAPTER 6**

Interviewing

So you've thrown out your net, recruited, found as many candidates to consider as possible, evaluated their initial responses, screened them, and determined if they should move to the next level. Interviewing is where the rubber hits the road. But now, instead of trying to draw people in, the purpose shifts to screening people out. Your job now is to find the ideal candidate.

The biggest mistake that interviewers make is that they talk too much. An interviewer should only talk about 20 percent of the time. This is the candidate's opportunity to shine. I think the reason that interviewers talk too much is that they're nervous, so be prepared. Know what you're doing before you walk into that room. Know what you're going to say, what questions you're going to ask, and what you're looking for.

Another mistake I see people make is trying to make friends with candidates instead of truly interviewing them. Everyone wants to be liked, but that's truly not the focus of what you're doing here. Be professional and pleasant, but don't try to be the candidate's buddy. There are a number of interview styles that can be employed to reveal different characteristics and skills. If you know what you want to learn before you go into the interview process, you can craft the interviews to help you expose those things, both good and bad.

A *one-on-one interview* is the traditional method where the candidate meets alone with the interviewer. Questions are asked by both parties to determine whether or not it's a good fit and whether the candidate fulfills the hard and soft requirements of the position.

Group interviews are helpful in certain circumstances where you might want to see how someone functions as part of a team or in a group environment. Or you may need to find multiple candidates for a single job description, like a position in retail sales or food service. Group interviews are also an effective tool at finding upper-level candidates, as this interview style often reveals who demonstrates natural leadership and/or diplomacy skills.

A *stress interview* is a high-pressure situation that reveals how a candidate may react in a tense environment. I highly recommend these for salespeople, as a test of skill and effectiveness under pressure. In a stress interview, you keep drilling down on one thing, searching for a breaking point.

Here's an example of a stress interview: I had a candidate come in, and I wanted to know what her prior year W-2 was. She kept talking about her earning potential and how she was successful at this and how she was successful at that. I said, "Great, but I asked you specifically about your 2012 W-2. What was it?" Again, on and on she went. "Stop right there," I said. "You're not answering my question. What was your 2012 W-2?" I was very insistent and very rapid-fire in my questioning, which was very similar to the sales environment we were interviewing for. Instead of answering my question, she called me a bitch. I made a note that she would not do well in a stressful sales environment.

Rote interviews are very "yes and no." You ask a series of questions, looking for specific answers. "Can you type?" Yes. "Can you work

8:00 to 5:00?" Yes. "Can you make a chart in Excel?" I don't know, but I'm good with computers. "Have you answered phones before?" Yes. "Can you start Monday?" Yes. "Great, you've got the job, and we'll train you in Excel."

A *behavioral interview* is the exact opposite of the rote method. Instead of asking yes and no questions, use questions that require the candidate to talk, describe, and explain. It's basically a conversation designed to discover if candidates have the hard and soft skills you need.

I generally start out all my behavioral interviews with, "I'm going to go through a couple questions because I want to better understand your background." And that's exactly what a behavioral interview is: an attempt to better understand the candidate's background and fit.

If I need a detail-oriented person, I might ask, "Tell me about your career." If I have an individual that answers by taking me through his or her career progression in a logical path along a timeline, that is a sign to me that the candidate is a detail-oriented person. A creative thinker will likely answer by describing his or her favorite job first and working down the list to his or her least favorite job. The behavioral interview has revealed that this candidate may not be the kind of detail-oriented person I'm looking for but that he or she might be the perfect person to put in the advertising department.

As always, select your questions ahead of time, and ask each candidate the same questions. In a behavioral interview, your focus is on listening. You don't have time to think of what you'll say next. Let the questions guide you and consider if you need to probe a little deeper into candidates' answers.

In all forms of interviewing, having your questions in place beforehand is not only a great organizational strategy but a protective one.

If all candidates are asked the same questions, it will be harder to pursue any kind of discrimination claim about why someone did or did not get the job.

THE INTERVIEW PROCESS

All interviews, no matter what style, should follow this same simple pattern: the opening, the actual interview, the closing, and the evaluation.

When you first sit down to interview someone, you want to put him or her at ease. If you're nervous about interviewing, you may choose to break the ice by saying, "I'm a bit nervous too—I don't interview much." Revealing something small about yourself puts the other person at ease, as does giving them the big picture of what the interview process will be.

Let the candidate know that you're going to have a conversation: that you want to understand their background a little bit better, that you'll talk about the position, and that he or she will have an opportunity to ask you questions before talking about next steps. This describes the complete arc in full clarity.

Proceed through your interview, as planned, with your questions at the ready.

In closing an interview, make sure that all your questions have been answered and then ask, "What questions do you have for me?" Candidates can ask what I like about the company. They can ask why the position's open. I don't care what they ask as long as they ask me *something*. Asking a question demonstrates their interest in the job and shows that they were paying attention during the interview.

The only person I will excuse from asking me a question are candidates who were so clearly nervous in the interview that it would likely kill them to ask me a direct question.

When the interview is over, I'll say, "Thank you for coming in. We have several interviews scheduled, but we anticipate making a decision and moving on to the second round of interviews by this time next week." I let them know what the next steps are and then stand, shake their hand, and gesture toward the door.

It's critical to evaluate the interview before moving on to the next candidate. Fill out your chart and mark your boxes. For example, you may have been looking for three soft skills: dependability, customer service, and detail orientation. Write the numbers directly into your chart. Do this before you pick up your smartphone, before you look at your e-mail, and before you answer your voicemail.

Don't skip this step! The interview isn't really over until the candidate has left and you have finished recording your evaluation into your chart. Even if you're a trained, skilled interviewer, if you have three interviews in one day and wait until the end of the day to evaluate them, you are not going to remember with total clarity who said what. Evaluate the candidate and set the paper aside until you are completely finished with the interviewing process.

WHEN THINGS GO WRONG

There are a lot of things that can go wrong during an interview that are difficult to defend later. Perhaps you don't have any notes from the interview. Perhaps you do have notes, but they show that you asked every candidate a different set of questions or spent hugely varied amounts of time with people.

For example, maybe you only spent a couple minutes with one candidate, and you ended up hiring him because he was Uncle James's second cousin. But you spent a full ten minutes with the minority candidate that you *didn't* actually consider, and for seven of those minutes, all you did was talk. You didn't ask any questions. You didn't allow that candidate the opportunity to demonstrate that he or she was or was not qualified.

With the correct process in place, however, you're protected. It gives you a way to let down Uncle James's second cousin, because you can say, "We treated you the same way we did everybody else, and the person we hired is just a better fit. We'll try to find you something in the organization." This also gives you an out with Uncle James, because you have quantifiable evidence as to why you hired someone other than his second cousin. You can explain that you can't hire based on nepotism (or cronyism, or any "-ism") and that his cousin wasn't going to be successful in that particular position.

Most of all, having a correct process protects you from *you*. We are our own worst enemies: We talk too much in interviews. We collect people who are more like us than they are actually qualified. But this is all human nature, and as long as we realize where these fallacies and errors are in our selections, we can correct them.

When we take time to prepare for our interviews and use the same job-related questions and format with every applicant, we reveal similarities and differences in candidate responses that are easier to compare and contrast. Instead of responding emotionally, we can make a thoughtful, balanced decision about who is truly best for the job, often surprising ourselves with our final choice.

 **CHAPTER 7**

Selection

Selecting the right candidate is an agonizing process, right? It's impossible to know from the interview how someone will actually behave in his or her job, right? Wrong.

When you're finished interviewing all potential candidates, pull out all of those evaluation sheets that you set aside and sort them from highest to lowest. Look at the person on the top of the stack. That's the candidate you hire.

If you followed best practices, kept your documentation and tracking going all along, and have your evaluation forms, then the process should have made your selection for you. Let the process work for you, and trust it. You may be lead to a surprisingly good match.

That doesn't mean you shouldn't do your due diligence before giving the top candidate a formal offer. Checking references is an important step in determining your final candidate and should be done before the offer is made. I tend to check references for only my top two or three candidates, but I never skip this step.

Always ask for professional references (not personal references) and recognize that candidates are going to give you names of people who will speak favorably of them. Nine out of ten times, the person giving the reference is going to give you the candidate's name, rank, and serial number only. Everyone is a little afraid to provide references because they don't want to be sued for saying the wrong thing. But if you listen closely to tone and to what information is provided, you can get much of the information you need.

HR INSIDER TIP: PRIOR EMPLOYER

Instead of asking candidates for permission to speak to a specific person, ask for permission to speak with their *prior employer*. Once you get that permission, you're cleared to talk to anyone from their immediate supervisor to their old CEO. Instead of talking to the reference candidates provide, you might try to find out who their immediate managers were and go directly to them.

MAKING THE OFFER

Once you make your selection, you can make the offer—but don't jump the gun and reject your other candidates yet. Wait until your offer has been accepted before you let everyone else down. It's awfully embarrassing to have to go back to the number-two candidate and say, "I know I rejected you yesterday, but I really want you to come work for me today."

I always recommend a phone call offer. I also believe that, in an ideal world, the hiring manager should make the offer. That way, the manager starts developing a relationship with his or her new employee right away. If that's not an option, then use your best judgment in selecting who makes the offer.

Follow the phone call with an offer letter to ensure clarity. You want to make sure that everything's perfectly understood. "Here's your at-will employment offer, here's your job title, here's what your pay rate's going to be, here's your starting date, and here's where you report to." In doing this, we're setting safe boundaries and further developing those new relationships. Be sure the offer is "contingent upon successfully completing" any other necessary requirements, such as a background check or drug testing.

Be cautious when asking the new employee to sign the offer letter and return it. Be sure you haven't created a contract. An offer letter should include at-will employment and be a description of your company's terms, what you've talked about, and what's involved. It's also more branding: you're bringing the person into the fold.

After the contingent offer is made—but before you fully employ the candidate—you should run a background check and/or perform any other pre-employment, post-offer tests to confirm that you can, in good faith, employ that person without putting your employees or clients in jeopardy.

You shouldn't necessarily run a background check for everyone. For one thing, there's a cost involved. There are also some state and/or local laws that may prohibit completing a background check until you have made an offer of employment. The background check that you run also has to be tied to the job that the subject will be doing. There has to be a *bona fide occupational qualification* (BFOQ) attached.

For example, there's no reason to run a credit check on a receptionist, a machinist, or someone in accounts payable. Their credit has no bearing on their ability to do their jobs. However, if you're hiring a bank teller, that person is handling your money and your customers' money. While a history of credit issues won't tell you if candidates will steal or not, bad credit does indicate a higher risk that they might be tempted to help themselves to a couple dollars here or there.

If your credit check reveals poor credit, it's your duty to look into *why*. Poor credit may not discount a candidate from the job (it might even be part of the reason why he or she needs it), but do look into it and have a conversation with the candidate. Losing your job and defaulting on your student loans is different than maxing out three new credit cards for a trip to Tahiti. I wouldn't worry if a candidate fell behind on medical bills after a one-time event, but I would raise an eyebrow if someone has fifteen credit cards, all of which are currently over the limit. Remember that the Fair Credit Reporting Act and other state laws may apply.

Background checks have been considered a consumer report for some time now, which means that they fall under the Fair Credit Reporting Act.[4] If you are doing a background check of any kind, you must provide the individual with a copy of their rights under the Fair Credit Reporting Act. This is because there are certain steps that you are required to take if you are going to take a negative or adverse action against an individual because of information that you received through a background check (such as not hiring that individual).

---

4 Federal Trade Commission. Lesley Fair. "Keep FCRA in the foreground when the subject is background screening." Last modified April 9, 2014. https://www.ftc.gov/news-events/blogs/business-blog/2014/04/keep-fcra-foreground-when-subject-background-screening.

HR INSIDER TIP: BAN THE BOX REGULATIONS

"Ban the Box" regulations cover that one little area on job applications where you are asked, "Have you ever been convicted of a crime?"

In some states and municipalities, "Ban the Box" regulations require employers to remove criminal record-related questions from job applications. Does this mean that I can't check someone's criminal record in the future? It does not. If there's a BFOQ (Bona Fide Occupational Qualification) for me to check a reference, I can and will check the person's background when the time is appropriate. But do I need to know if candidates have been convicted of a crime *before* I interview them? In all honesty, probably not. Until they're my employees—or are about to be—that's their personal business.

When looking at a criminal record report, look only at pertinent information from the past seven years. Unfortunately, some criminal reports show everything—it's hard to not look, but ignore it if it's not relevant to the job!

If I see a felony theft charge on someone I'm hiring for a retail operation, then the offer will probably be rescinded after following the EEOC's recommended analysis. However, if the individual has a misdemeanor charge for damage of personal goods, I'm going to have a conversation with him or her in order to better understand the situation.

I once interviewed a twenty-year-old woman who was an ideal candidate for a position, but her background check revealed some charges that were a little questionable for a retail environment. When I had a conversation with her, she told me what happened. In high school, her friends dared her to steal a stick of lip gloss. She took the dare and was caught. Because she was over 18, it went on her record. Embarrassed, she told me she'd learned her lesson and that she now understands that your actions and their consequences follow you. After that conversation, there was no reason not to bring her on board. She's now an awesome employee! But if I had not had that conversation with her, I likely would have skipped over her and moved on to someone else.

You may ask yourself, "Why do a background check at all?" The main reason is to protect yourself from something called *negligent hiring*. Imagine that I'm hiring a service technician to go into people's homes. I fail to do a background check and unwittingly hire someone convicted for armed robbery. He goes into my customer's house, cases the house during the install, and then returns later that night and robs them blind. That family can now sue me, the employer, for negligent hiring—and they should. I didn't do my due diligence and failed to protect my customers.

REJECTIONS

Be careful how you reject someone. That person might be a future customer or a future hire, and if you don't reject him or her nicely, you could lose that potential. Plus, social media—need I say more?

Imagine that your number-two candidate for a sales job would actually be ideal in customer service, and next week, you have a customer service position open up. You can simply skip a second hiring process and call that person to see if he or she is interested. But if the rejection was handled poorly, that person may say, "Um … no thanks. I don't want to work for you."

Treat everyone you interview as a potential future candidate or customer. Even if they're not right for the job, they may still be good for your business.

 **CHAPTER 8**

Orientation and Onboarding

Onboarding is the latest buzzword and with good reason. Onboarding allows for employees to take some time to get up to speed, helping them to become rock stars at their jobs. In an ideal world, onboarding would start with the offer letter, continue through the start date, and keep going, but there's a huge disconnect with how much of an orientation period is offered and what is actually needed. Unfortunately, most orientations for new employees consist of an hour spent with HR filling out paperwork, and from there we send them off with their business cards and say, "go get 'em!" However, when you look at the chart below, you can see we are doing a great disservice to new employees by not giving them adequate time and training to acclimate and thoroughly learn their new position.

Time it takes a new employee to fully embrace their new position
General employee: 6–9 months, up to a year
Supervisor: 12–18 months
Manager: 1.5–2 years

Think about the last time you changed jobs and how nerve-wracking day one was. Think of what you can do ahead of time to onboard new employees and to make them less nervous about day one. It could be as simple as showing them where they should park when they arrive, talking to them about what people generally wear to work or recommending where to eat lunch.

The week before new employees start, you might give them a tour of the building and facilities, including restrooms and fire escapes. You might give them a walking tour of the surrounding area, pointing out nearby restaurants and services. You could provide a packet with an overview of the company perks and benefits, a list of the job descriptions, or a chart showing how departments and positions are interrelated. You could send them training or orientation schedules so they can ask questions before arriving.

The more we address the little stuff ahead of time, the more at ease new hires will be when they walk through that door, and the more we can get right into the meat of their job responsibilities on the very first day. Remember, your employees will be getting an orientation from someone. Make sure that someone is you and not the disgruntled accountant who lurks around the water cooler.

As new employees acclimate, follow up with them. Ask them how everything's going and listen to them sincerely. Is there anything you could've done better for them that first week? How can you help them be more comfortable next week?

With health care and benefits needing to be in place by the ninetieth day, a lot of companies have converted to a sixty-day orientation/introductory period to conclude before the benefit-waiting period ends.

Having an orientation/introductory period longer than ninety days defeats the purpose of a trial period. Regardless of the length of time, be sure to take advantage of this period. If new employees are right for you, you'll know. If not, move them along or move them out.

Make sure new employees have exposure to all of the jobs in the organization so that they understand how their position fits into the big picture. You can break your orientation down and start that with, "Here's our organization, mission, vision, and values. Here's the department you work in. Here's how your department fits into everything." Then funnel that down to, "Here's why your position is important. Here's why you are vital to our success." Make them feel like part of the team.

While the squeaky wheel demands the most oil, While squeaky wheel demands the most oil, the employees we *should* be spending the majority of our time on are the *good* employees—you know who they are, you can depend on them, and they embrace "all other duties as assigned!" Keep them on board and feeling like part of your team. You don't want to risk having them drop down to being unhappy and/or unchallenged, because you're not paying any attention to them. These employees get tired of being the go-to people. They get tired of being the ones that pick up after everybody else. Instead of spending 80 percent of your time with the less-than-stellar employees, flip that around and invest time in your superstars.

I think you'll find that your employees will get better at their jobs, faster, if you don't expect them to do everything out of the gate. Instead, walk them through a defined process. Don't throw them to the wolves, saying, "You've got the job, go do it."

If you have current employees who were never given orientations, you can still bring them on board. Treat them almost as if they're new employees. Naturally, you don't need to do the new employee paperwork, but you can have staff meetings where you walk through the onboarding process one section at a time, department by department, giving everyone a wider sense of the organization.

If your business has a slower period, take employees from one department and have them shadow in another department. Do this for half a day or even just an hour. Let them walk in their coworkers' shoes for a period of time. Let the warehouse person hear firsthand what it's like when a customer's calling and yelling, "I didn't get my toilet paper today! You sent me paper towels instead of toilet paper!"

So often, I hear supervisors say, "I can't wait until this group turns over and we can start again from scratch." But that's magical thinking. Unless everyone is fired (or quits) on the same day and you hire a completely new team, you never start from scratch. Just like having a starter for sourdough bread, that original culture stays with you. Forever. Fixing the recipe is up to the chef.

PART 3

Running The Ship

 **CHAPTER 9**

Employee Relations

People generally equate employee relations with a union environment. But really, it's your relationship with your employees. What kind of a relationship do you want to have? For example, if you say that you have an open-door policy, but every time an employee walks down your hall, they see that your door is closed, what message are you actually sending?

In your employee relations philosophy, actions always speak louder than words. I can pull in any number of catchphrases to illustrate this, but it all boils down to *doing what you say you're going to do when you say you're going to do it.* If you say you are going to get back to an employee on such-and-such, then get back to him or her about such-and-such.

Employee relations are also how you gain the respect of your employees. They don't have to agree with every decision you make, but if you have solid employee relations, they will respect your decisions. Respect is not granted along with your title; it's earned when you consistently demonstrate the mission, vision, and values of the organization. When you live your mission statement on a daily basis, you provide clarity in your actions and words. Everyone else will follow suit.

Maintaining good employee relations is a good way to show your employees that you respect them. If they have to live within the guidelines you set forth, they need to know that you're going to join them and lead the way. You should be beyond reproach—at least, as much as is humanly possible.

One of our core values at HR Resolutions is "going the second mile for clients is second nature." If I'm not demonstrating this value in every interaction I have with our clients, what message am I sending to my employees? I'm teaching them that they don't have to go the second mile, either. If you want people to come to work on time, then you should be the first one there, greeting your employees as they come in. *You* determine the corporate culture.

Your ability or inability to set boundaries has a huge effect on your employees. If they see you playing favorites or being especially hard on someone, they are going to do one of two things. They might distance themselves from the pet or pariah, thereby isolating themselves from the problem, or they might try to insinuate themselves into the relationship in order to curry favor.

When healthy employee relations are in place, you know to praise publicly and criticize privately. You know when to keep a conversation private and when to celebrate a team success.

LABOR RELATIONS

Labor relations have to do with a union environment. I've worked in both union and nonunion companies, and there is a difference between them. In a union environment, my rules are absolutely black and white. In a nonunion environment, my rules are gray. There are pros and cons to both types of environment, but the horrible, awful thing about union management is when the union first tries to get started in your organization. That can be a time of great confusion and high emotions. Employees are torn between their employer, whom they know, and the union, which may be promising the world. The employer is probably angry because some employee sought outside help; the employer may also be scared because they can't deliver everything that the union is promising. And no one is talking to anyone else!

There is a practice that all managers, supervisors, and leads should learn. It's called TIPS or SPIT—I prefer TIPS because it sounds nicer. If you get wind that a union is trying to rally your employees, it's *critical* that you and your supervisors understand these four things:

T—Do not **T**hreaten your employees. Don't say, "If you talk to the union, I will fire you."

I—Do not **I**nterrogate. Don't say, "Who was at that union meeting last night? Were you involved? Who said what?"

P—Don't **P**romise. Don't promise things you can't deliver, saying, "If you vote against the union, we'll give everybody a one-dollar-an-hour raise."

S—Don't do **S**urveillance. If you find out that the union organizers are meeting with some of your people down at the local Elks Lodge, *do not* go to the local Elks Lodge, take pictures of the license plates in the parking lot, and snap photos of who's going in and out.

In all honestly, I understand why certain employers would be terrified of their workers forming or joining a union. On a human level, it makes sense to try to fix the problem, saying, "We'll do better! You don't need a union—we'll fix what you don't like!" But once the union is involved, it's too late. You should've done all that before your employees went and spoke to a third party.

Once you believe that a union is talking to your employees, it is critical that you and your supervisors follow the four points of TIPS. If you don't follow even one of those four points, there is every likelihood that the NLRB will come to you and say, "Congratulations, you don't need to have a union election, because you violated your employees' rights. We've already told the union that they now represent your employees." That's how serious those four steps are.

In all of this, unions are not always a bad thing. They can help your employees organize and clarify their rights and needs, and they can be partners with you—advocating for your employees and speaking up as problems or issues arise. Unions can also make things really difficult for you, especially if you're not being good to your workers. So follow your best-practice guidelines, and step with foresight and care.

The bottom line: Treat your employees fairly. If you're fair, consistent, and live your mission statement, then employees may not like the decisions you make, but they will respect those decisions and give you the benefit of the doubt.

 **CHAPTER 10**

Payroll

A well-run payroll is a critical component of keeping your employees happy and feeling like they're in good hands. Besides that, the law requires you to pay people for the work that they've done for you. Your engaged employees might seem like they're working for you for fun, but they're not. There is a paycheck involved.

Take me, for example: I love human resources. I love what we do for our clients. I wish I could give it away for free, but I have people and rent that I have to pay. My passion doesn't write those checks, and it's the same for your employees. A paycheck is what makes it possible for them to live in America, to buy food and clothes, to educate their children, and to commute to the place where they work for *you*.

Sometimes, making payroll work for you means outsourcing it to another company. Outsourcing the payroll takes away a number of concerns that may not be part of your expertise, such as properly calculating tax liabilities. While there is an expense to outsourcing the payroll, you save in other ways—namely, time. Trust me, not having to sit down, figure out, and remit my quarterly and payroll taxes is heaven.

Of course, even if you're outsourcing payroll, someone in your organization still has to process the paychecks; but personally, I want someone else making those direct deposits. I don't want to be responsible for having to transfer money from my account into four separate accounts for my employees (or sixteen separate accounts or one hundred separate accounts). I want to make *one* transfer to the payroll company and let their employees deal with it. And if they screw up, the problem is theirs.

At the end of the day, it really comes down to tax liability and properly processing taxes. I could pay my accountant to handle it or do it myself, but under those circumstances, I still have liability if it's done incorrectly. And if I'm liable, then I pay any fines, taxes, and penalties. But if I hire a payroll company to do the taxes and they are done wrong, then that company is liable, and it has the responsibility to talk to the IRS or the local tax representative. That, in itself, is well worth the expense!

PAYROLL ERRORS: WHEN THINGS GO WRONG

Payroll errors happen—after all, you're only human. How you respond and how quickly and thoroughly you respond are what matter.

If you haven't been paying properly, fix it—and fix it before a government agency comes in and tells you to fix it, because then you'll be fixing it for a lot more people and for a lot longer. If you make two or three payroll errors in a row, or even close together, employees are going to get worried. They're going to ask, "What else are they not doing right?" That can lead to deeper concerns where they ask, "If they can mess this up, what else are they not doing right for our customers? What else are they not paying attention to in our company? Isn't this important to them? Am I not important to them?"

This is another solid reason why it's great to have a payroll service handle everything. You won't be the target if something goes wrong; instead, you'll be helping to solve it.

From time to time, an error is made in your employees' favor, like a larger amount of pay on one of their checks. Contrary to the employees' hopes and dreams, that error does not set a precedent. All errors should and must be corrected immediately.

If an error has been made in your employees' favor, your first thought might be, "Why didn't they notice this and come to me?" Maybe they did notice and kept it to themselves, but it's more likely they didn't notice, deposited the check as normal, and moved on. As frustrating as this is, if you didn't notice it, why should they?

As soon as you pinpoint the payroll error, I encourage you to sit down and have an open conversation with the employee. For example, you could say, "If you notice, here, for the last four paychecks, we paid you a dollar more per hour than what we had agreed upon. We can do a couple things here, but I'm sure you would agree that the company needs to get that money back."

Now, brace yourself, because employees are likely to say, "Well, you made the mistake and that money is gone." Take a breath and reply, "Absolutely, we made the mistake, but let's look at it this way: If I had underpaid you by one dollar, wouldn't you want your money? It's the exact same thing on our side. We need that money to pay your coworkers and to help this business grow. I wish we could let you keep that money, but it has already been spoken for in our budget."

At this point, you should come up with a repayment agreement with them. For example, you might adjust their payroll by lowering their pay to one dollar below their agreed upon hourly wage for the next four-page check to bring things in balance. (This works as long as you're still paying over minimum wage on the reduced salary—you always have to stay true to the wage and hour law.)

Remind the employees that you're not taking anything away from them. It's simply an issue of, "We paid you a little too much, and now we're going to smooth it back over. You're not actually making less over the course of the year."

Another thing that happens with some frequency is that an employer under-withholds their employees' benefits. Again, in most circumstances, you are entitled to reclaim that money. The employee signed up for benefits and understands that there was a cost to those benefits; they have signed an enrollment form that says, "You may withhold x from my paycheck," and therefore, you have every right and responsibility to bring things into alignment.

There may be occasions where you decide to let things go. You may say, "You know what? We're going to let you keep the extra money, not because we have to, but because it's a simple fix. We're going to correct the error going forward and put things back the way they should be."

The main thing is to always have the conversation. Don't just make an adjustment or let your employees keep extra funds without telling them why, what happened, and how you're correcting the situation.

BEYOND THE PAYCHECK: TOTAL COMPENSATION

While not exactly part of payroll, many of the contributions and deductions included in your employees' total compensation packages are processed through payroll.

We don't talk enough about total compensation. Employees get much more than a paycheck from us. Total compensation is something that we should be singing from the mountaintops. It includes any statutory compensation, benefits, workers' compensation, Social Security (sometimes known as old age, survivor, and disability insurance, or OASDI), and Medicare.

It's good to remind employees that we pay into those government-mandated insurance accounts for them—and these programs *are* insurances. For example, we provide workers' compensation insurance for them at no charge. All we ask in return is that they be safe on the job. You pay disability insurance so that if they get sick or hurt, you can continue to contribute financially to their household as they heal. There are medical, dental, and vision benefits. There are vacation days, sick days, and more.

It's well worth your time to add what you're paying for all the included benefits you provide and show your employees their percentage of the cost. Explain how the amount you pay is *in addition* to the wages on their paycheck. They may be pleasantly surprised to see how much you're paying to keep them safe and protected. And later, when they're retired, they'll be able to pull a modest salary from Social Security, which is being paid into their OASDI account every paycheck.

Supplemental benefits include things like 401(k)s, simple IRAs, and any voluntary insurance like Aflac, Colonial Life, and Allstate, if you want to provide those things. Many of these benefits are completely employee-funded (except for any retirement funding match), but you should still point out the fact that as an employer, you make these plans available to them, for their choice.

There are also ways that your employees save on everyday things by coming to the office five days a week, and these small savings can actually add up to a big chunk of change by the end of the year. For example, if you have free coffee in the break room every day, thus saving your employees a daily trip to Starbucks, you could be saving them $5–$10 a day. Five days a week, fifty-two weeks a year (minus two for vacation)—that's a savings of $1,250–$2,500 in coffee alone. Add in free lunch on Fridays at a cost of about $15 per employee, and they save another $750 on lunch. Get the picture?

Beyond the break room, there are company picnics and parties, paid time off, subsidized pre-tax metro cards, and use of the copy machine and paper. All those things add up and are of financial benefit to your workers.

THE DEVIL'S IN THE DETAILS

Believe me, your employees are paying attention to their paychecks, so it's well worth your while to get the details in order.

A human resource information system (HRIS) is a database that captures any and every piece of information about your employee—age, race, emergency contact information, benefits enrollment, dependent information. Any data that you may need to access on an individual can be housed in an HRIS system.

Do you really need a system like that? Probably not. If you've already outsourced your payroll, there is probably a field somewhere in that payroll system that is related to whatever data you need to track. Similarly, it's unlikely that you'll need an HR software program.

For example, if you need to track gender for some reason, you can bet there's a field in the payroll for an employee's gender. There may not, however, be a field for Equal Employment Opportunity (EEO) classification.

EEO classification is the category or type of work that an individual does, based upon nine categories of employment. There are nine categories, each detailed in the table below.

EEO CLASSIFICATION
0-1 is management
0-2, professionals
0-3, technicians
0-4, sales
0-5, clerical
0-6, skilled
0-7, semi-skilled
0-8, unskilled
0-9, labor

Here's when EEO classifications come into play: if you need to do any type of government work, you may be asked to classify what ethnicities you have employed in each job classification. You may also need to disclose this information if you're applying for any grants, federal programs, or subsidies.

You may also need to track your employees' disability and/or veteran status, which probably don't have corresponding fields in your payroll system. But again, if this status is something you need to track, your payroll company can help you find a category in the system that you can rename (or create a new one) to track this data.

One thing that you most definitely have to track is Section 125 of the Internal Revenue Code. This is the tax code that allows employers to withhold certain benefits on a pre-tax basis. You are required to have an actual written plan document of your Section 125 benefits.

It's a straightforward document, but it has to be done accurately. There is a cost to creating this document, but some supplemental insurance carriers like Aflac, Colonial Life, and Allstate will do it for free as an added bonus for offering their benefits.

Employers also have a duty to explain to employees that anything done pre-tax *does* have an impact on their Social Security and Medicare funds. It's a small impact, but we have a responsibility to disclose the information. We also have a responsibility to explain that Section 125 is also the law that determines when we can allow individuals to enter and exit the insurance plans in the middle of year.

If the enrollment date has passed, there needs to be a family status change or a life event to go on or off a plan in the middle of a year. (Qualifying family members include spouses and dependents.) In the Section 125 plan document, we define what these life events are. The IRS also has a list that basically boils down to marital status change, dependent status change, or a change in your eligibility—that is, either you're no longer eligible for benefits because of the hours that you work or you've become eligible for benefits because of the hours you work.

TROUBLESHOOTING

Whether your payroll processes are in-house or outsourced, you should audit them periodically using what's called a *gross-to-net test*. Unfortunately, that means that you may have to go to the IRS to get the tax tables and figure out various issues. If that's too much of a hassle, you can do a *thumbprint check*, which is where you take the employee's gross wages and subtract everything that was withheld. Does it come out to the net amount? If it does, you're done. If not, investigate further.

The reason you go through all this is to demonstrate to an auditor that you pay attention to your payroll. It also helps you check for errors, like accidentally paying someone extra wages. Before you even submit the payroll, make sure that all of your numbers balance. If they don't balance, figure out why *before* you process checks, when problems are easier to fix. During your internal audit, make sure that your paperwork matches your payroll. For example, if you have an individual marked with Federal Tax Exemptions of "single-0" on their paycheck, make sure that you have the backup of their W-4 that says they're claiming "single-0."

Depending on the size of your payroll, I recommend that you break it down and audit quarterly to avoid overwhelming yourself.

If an employee wants to change a deduction (for example, if they want to change their tax exemptions or their retirement plan withholding), don't accept a request via e-mail. Make sure they fill out the appropriate form. The IRS audits your tax withholdings and payroll against W-4 forms, and they will not accept an e-mail as a legitimate W-4. You must withhold based upon the legal W-4 document.

Knowing that payroll, a critical business component, is a well-oiled machine makes your employees confident about planning for the future and trusting that they will be taken care of properly.

 **CHAPTER 11**

Benefits Management

I think the important thing to remember is that benefits don't have to cost an arm and a leg. You've got your traditional benefits like medical, dental, and vision. Everybody thinks of those off the top of their head, but there are a lot of other benefits.

For example, a flexible work schedule is a benefit. When we interview people for our office and they ask what the office hours are, I say, "We come in any time between eight o'clock and nine o'clock, and we leave any time between four o'clock and six o'clock." Telecommuting is a benefit. Telecommuting and a flexible schedule don't cost me anything as an employer.

When you think about what you might offer outside the traditional benefits, it's smart to ask your employees what they would value. A flexible schedule may not be a good fit for detail-oriented thinkers. They may prefer parameters. A highly creative thinker might love a flexible schedule, but he or she might actually need a set schedule to get any work done. Something that's a benefit for one employee could be an irritant for another. It's up to you to find the balance.

While I don't necessarily talk about benefits when I'm first interviewing, I definitely talk about them when I'm bringing someone on board. Our benefits package is pretty standard, in order to ensure consistencies. You don't want to be accused of showing favoritism or offering something to someone because they're Caucasian and not offering the same thing to someone else because they're Asian. You have to be cautious of that, but you still have flexibility in developing a program that's right for both your company and your employees.

Look at your traditional benefits, and find an insurance broker that you trust implicitly. This is the person that is going to go shop your benefit plans for you. You want someone who has your best interests in mind.

You need a broker who is going to help you completely understand why one benefit package that might be a little bit more expensive is better than another benefit package, which might be a little less expensive but doesn't cover as much. Your broker needs to understand what your mission, vision, and values are. Your broker needs to have clarity about your organization so that he or she can best represent you out in the benefit marketplace. He or she is going to be a trusted resource for you.

You should also be able to rely on your broker to help troubleshoot when issues arise. Finding a good broker isn't so different from finding a good dentist, real estate agent, or tailor. Ask around. Trust your peers. Whom do they work with?

If you're unhappy with your current broker, you can always change. I don't recommend that you do so every year, because then you lose any continuity, but it's certainly better to find someone you respect and trust. I get phone calls all of the time from brokers who say, "Hey, I can get you a better deal." No they can't. Broker A, Broker B, and Broker C are going to get you the exact same rates from Blue Cross and Blue Shield or Aetna. The rates are the rates.

You need to be looking for trust, confidence, and someone whom you can rely upon. You need to be looking for the cultural fit, and you need to be looking at service. I have some brokers that are completely hands-off. They get you the quotes, you sign them, and they say, "We'll see you next year when it's time for renewal." That's how they are. I have other brokers who partner with me through the entire year. They will come out for open enrollment meetings. They will speak directly with my employees if something goes beyond what I can address. They will be my advocate. They negotiate with my insurance carriers for me.

For example, we just had a plan where there was a twelve-month waiting period for major services. That was part of the plan for a long time, but it affected two newer employees this year when they had to dip into their own pockets. That is contradictory to my philosophy of taking care of my employees. The broker stepped in and renegotiated the plan. It was good timing, because we were just preparing for open enrollment, enabling us to share this with employees in a timely manner. He negotiated to do away with that waiting period, and it only cost us seventy-five cents per employee, per month.

On an aside, I have one broker who spoils me terribly, and it's wonderful. I wish I could model all my other brokers after this one. The staff put together all my paperwork for open enrollment. I even get calls from our customer service agent every month, checking in. I have very little that I have to handle other than getting paperwork back from employees. Because of this fantastic service, I'll never switch to another broker; this benefits my employees in the long run through continuity and interpersonal relationships. They get good service, and they feel good about it, too.

Other partners, who are often overlooked, are your financial planners. They assist with any retirement plans you may offer. They're not necessarily brokers, but you want to have someone who is available to speak with your employees, help them make decisions, and describe options to them. That's not something you want to be responsible for.

There are many fiduciary responsibilities when you offer a retirement plan. Some of the fiduciary responsibilities are: you have to provide regular education about retirement, you have to review your overall plan once every so many years, and you should have an investment committee that evaluates the funds that you are making available for your plan. Depending upon the type of plan, you have more or fewer responsibilities. With a traditional 401(k), you probably have the maximum amount of fiduciary responsibilities. You have to audit it every year and evaluate the plan annually. 401(k)s are highly regulated.

THE BENEFITS OF BENEFITS

Offering benefits is one way in which you can set yourself apart from other employers. More and more employers offer benefits to their part-timers. They want quality workers who stay for years—and they get them. Benefits make a difference with recruiting quality workers, and they make a difference with retention.

The Employee Retirement Income Security Act (ERISA) is a big regulatory legislation that protects our employees and their benefits. Imagine withholding money for medical benefits from your employees but not paying the insurance premiums. Your employees are under the impression that they've had insurance all this time, but when they go to the doctor, their claims are denied because their insurance was cancelled. Or imagine that you've withheld your employees' retirement money, but you never made the matching contributions that you promised, so there's no company money going into their IRAs or

401(k)s. Not only did you fail to remit the money to their retirement funds, but they also lost any money they would've earned from interest.

If you've done anything like the above examples, you will be found out. You will get a letter from the DOL (specifically, the ERISA division) saying, "Dear Employer, please help us to understand whatever it is that's going on. *Certainly* you have not intended to do this, because doing this would be committing fraud."

Besides having angry employees, there can be nasty fines and penalties involved. Not only do you have to pay back the money that you already withheld (which was their money anyway), but you have to spend time, effort, and energy to figure out the interest that they would have earned, which you must also pay back. Finally, you have to pay fines and penalties to the government. That's what happens when you don't pay attention to your benefits. This is not your money to play around with or ignore.

The best companies to work for are differentiating themselves based on employee relations and *perks*. Anybody can offer medical, dental, and vision. Not everybody can or does offer flexible benefits. Not everybody can or does offer a lending library or shade-grown coffee in the break room like Zappos does. It's actually interesting reading (check out fortune.com/best-companies)—you never know what you may be able to offer that you had never considered!

Perks are funded entirely by employers, with no employee contribution. They're not insurance. They're not backed by another company. They're just extra things that we choose to give our employees to set ourselves apart from our competitors or to align our culture with our mission, vision, and values.

Places like Google and Spotify have perks that seem unbelievable—free meals and snacks, standing desks and yoga ball chairs, nap rooms and game rooms. But the perks make sense when you consider that those companies are looking to draw workers who will think of the office as their home (and will stay there around the clock). New Belgium Brewing Company, in Fort Collins, Colorado, gives employees a new bike after they've worked there for a certain number of months, and it hosts free movie nights out on its big front lawn. New Belgium is looking to draw employees who value being eco-friendly and who enjoy a communal atmosphere. While these companies draw different kinds of people, *they each draw the right kind of people for that company.* And not surprisingly, their employees generally *love* to go to work.

Places like libraries have perks like rows and rows of free books that you can read during quiet hours—this is completely free to the library, but it's a big draw to people who choose to become librarians. Find what works for you and what excites your employees.

SAMPLE COMMON PERKS:

- A corner office with windows
- A larger-than-normal office
- A nice, ergonomic chair
- A break room stocked with snacks
- A pre-tax commuter card
- Free lunch once a month
- Summer hours
- Permission to bring your pets to work
- Product/service discounts

You may not realize how many perks you're already offering to your employees. Point them out at the next meeting. Be proud. Show your employees that they're getting lots of great stuff, just because you feel like they deserve it and want them to be happy.

Offering perks can save you time and money in the long run because they can help minimize your turnover and add to workplace satisfaction. A little goes a long way.

When we talk about what a good place to work looks like, we're talking about a place where your employees feel protected, are able to plan for their future, and are also able to take care of themselves and their families. With the perks you offer, they'll probably be able to have some work-life balance.

As your employees come to understand that you truly have their best interests at heart, the bonds of loyalty and security grow. Overall, benefits management comes down to doing the right thing for the people who are under your care. That's one of HR Resolution's core values: Do the right thing, always. It may not always be easy or cheap, but it's never wrong.

 **CHAPTER 12**

Safety

In this chapter, we'll focus on creating a physically safe environment, starting with company culture and awareness. It may come as a surprise, but 95 percent of workplace accidents are the result of an unsafe behavior, which is a cultural problem, rather than an unsafe physical space.

For example, a file cabinet is not unsafe in and of itself. But if an employee is in a rush and leaves the drawer open, that *behavior* of not closing the drawer creates a hazard. If your employee was feeling rushed, then you have a responsibility to correct that. Perhaps that person has too much work, perhaps he or she is overstressed, or perhaps there's a company culture of hurrying and always appearing to be busy. Whatever the cause, you want to create a space where your employees know that they can calmly walk to a file cabinet, get what they need, close it, go back to their desk, and trust that you're not going to be screaming at them to hurry up.

Aside from it being the right thing to do, providing a safe work environment is your duty as an employer. Referring back to OSHA, their General Duty Clause states that we have the duty to maintain a workplace that is free of hazards.

To do that, you have to think like someone who is walking into the environment for the first time. You may be used to that heavy door that swings shut really quickly and know to stop it with your foot before it hits you in the face, but your new sales rep might not know that. Go through with fresh eyes (or bring in someone new to walk through the building with you), and fix what needs to be fixed. Ask your employees if there's anything they've noticed, from a sharp corner on a desk that always rips their sleeve to a slick spot on the floor where the polish is extra slippery.

The best safety program is one that's built on education and awareness. DuPont practically wrote the book on workplace safety programs. There are many programs out there, but you don't even need to invest in one. All you need to do is talk about safety and to have your people talk about safety. If your employees see something that is unsafe, have them fix it, even if it's not in their department. Make it a company policy that if you see a spill on the floor, then you clean it up—even if you didn't cause the spill.

Make sure that your employees know that they can come to you when something is broken, without repercussions. If your equipment isn't working properly or is broken, or if an employee tells you that something is broken, fix it right away. That might seem obvious, but you'd be surprised how many people just put it off indefinitely with an "I'll get to it later" attitude. That *later* could come when someone gets seriously injured (which is bad enough on its own), and you're in court because you were well aware of the problem.

Fix it early, fix it often. If you wait and a problem gets worse, it's going to cost you more money to fix. But it goes beyond that; it's about a safe environment. I'll once again use my company, HR Resolutions, as an example. We used to have a traditional locking door with a deadbolt. My staff works upstairs in our building. If I'm not in the office, that means that the building was left open on the ground level. At one point, when we had an office space for rent, someone actually walked into the building, went all the way upstairs, and inquired about renting the office space. I had one woman working there at that time, and she was alone. Had the situation been even slightly different—had the person who walked in been someone with bad intentions—she could've been in danger. Within a week I had badge entry and a doorbell. Yes, it cost money, but it was my duty to make sure that my environment and my employees were safe.

TRAINING

There are certain safety training programs that should be conducted annually. One is so simple and so much fun that it's hard to understand why employers forget about it: fire extinguisher training. It's a blast, literally and figuratively. It also gives you an opportunity to connect with your community because your local fire department will probably do the training for only the cost of the chemical in the extinguisher. So not only are you helping the fire department by training your workers to put out fires, you're also making a contribution to your local fire company.

Another training subject that can be a lot of fun is evacuation training. For example, you can have somebody stand in an exit, blocking it and holding a little sign that says, "I'm fire!" I don't care what age you are—you learn better and remember for longer if you are enjoying yourself. Yes, fire extinguisher training and evacuation training are serious business, but you want people to have total recall. To do that, they need to have been paying attention during training.

As you're doing all this training, you're also passing on your company culture to your employees. You're showing that you take these things seriously but that you're not there to lecture. You want people to participate and take ownership in the training. I don't know how many office buildings I've visited where nobody moves when the fire alarms go off. People shrug and say, "Those alarms always go off." But someday, there could actually be a fire.

WORKERS' COMPENSATION

Something employees are uniquely attuned to is *workers' compensation.* Your responsibility will be workers' compensation *management.* If you have a workplace accident, you have a duty to investigate it so that you can prevent it from happening again. This is also a time to revisit the General Duty Clause. You have a responsibility to send your employees home whole and healthy. If they are hurt at work, you must return them to whole and healthy.

History and a lot of studies show that the sooner people get back to their regular routine, the sooner they will recover from a workplace injury. And with all due respect to my attorney friends, you don't want your injured employee at home watching TV and being bombarded with those ambulance-chaser commercials: "Hurt at work? Call us now!"

In all seriousness, if you want your employees to return to you whole and healthy, you don't want them to fall out of practice while sitting at home, collecting two-thirds of their paycheck. It can be very tempting for them to relax into that kind of routine.

Generally, my philosophy for work injury recovery is that unless you are in the hospital, you come to work. There is always something I can find for you to do as long as the employee is released to perform light duty work. However, I have to balance that mind-set against what is in the best interest of the individual healing and what is best for the safety of other employees.

For instance, if I have someone in a cast and on crutches, I probably don't want that person in the warehouse. But that doesn't mean there isn't work that injured employees can do. They can help in reception and greet people at the door. I can train them to answer phones or organize files. Whatever it is, I want to keep them an active part of my team. Psychologically, that's healthier for them, and it's certainly better for me to have someone who's pitching in, rather than one who's sitting at home.

When it comes to workers' compensation case management, you want to get involved and stay involved. After a workplace accident, there are going to be a number of different people involved: the injured employee, the employer, the insurance company, and the treating physician; the insurance company may even assign a nurse case manager to the claim. Everyone should be equally involved in the process. A lot of employers skip out on the process and just let the insurance company handle it, but all parties are best served when employers are actively involved in case management.

The more actively you are involved in the case from the start, the less likely it is that an attorney is going to come in. Once an attorney gets involved, you're out. You can still talk to the employee and you *should* talk to the employee about work—they're expected to return to work, and it is your duty to communicate that to the employee, attorney or no attorney—but you cannot talk to them at that point about the case. Saying something like, "Are you satisfied with your provider? Is everything going to your satisfaction?" is off-limits once a lawyer is involved. It's better to manage the case from start to finish.

Remember, the adjusters at the insurance company are not necessarily your advocates. They have a hundred other injured employees' cases to worry about, and they're looking to minimize the insurance company's costs. Ideally, they will welcome your involvement with the case management because you want to get the employee back to his or her regular duty as quickly as possible, which saves the insurance company money and takes a case off their docket.

Workers' compensation adjusters get a little nervous when you start saying things like, "You know what? They've been off work too long. I've got to move on," but you are not obligated to maintain a position for that person forever. You should follow your ADA and other leave and absence policies. If you have fifty or more employees, you should be putting your injured employee on FMLA. Start that twelve-week timer. It doesn't mean that at the end of twelve weeks, you're going to terminate the injured employee; it does mean that at the end of twelve weeks, you get to evaluate your options.

In case management, you should be constantly communicating with the insurance adjuster. Nothing should be a surprise to the adjuster, to the employee, or to you. If you need to move on, you need to move on. It will cost the insurance company more (and it will cost you more because it will impact your loss ratio and future rates), but you also can't hold a job for someone for two years—or should you. All the time you're holding that job, the injured employee is may be on your medical benefits program. They're not an active employee, so technically you may be violating your contract with your medical insurance company. There are so many pieces that have to be juggled, so manage claims from the start and don't stop until they're resolved.

THE BENEFITS OF
DOING THINGS RIGHT

When good safety management is truly in place, you'll see a lot more teamwork. Instead of just managers watching other employees' backs, other employees will watch out for each other and help more often. If you've done things right, your employees are actually running your safety awareness program for you, saying, "Hey Johnny, you didn't have your seatbelt fastened when you were on your forklift. Gotta buckle up, man!" Your employees will pick up on the education and awareness and will weave it into their culture.

With good safety management, you'll also see a kind of generosity of spirit and awareness that is self-regulating and protective. For example, if somebody's getting a box down, a coworker is right there, saying, "Here, let me help you. Let's make sure you're not standing on a rickety chair." Employees have a better understanding of how their actions impact others—they know that if Carla in accounts payable goes down, they're going to have to trust a temp to get those checks out on time.

Finally, when everything is running smoothly, you'll have a great relationship with your adjusters if there *is* an injury. Make sure the adjusters know that you're there to make their jobs easier. We generally think that adjusters should make *our* lives easier, but you have to work together. Just remember—they've got a lot of work on their desks, too. They're just people, and they are also people who can really help you when you need it.

An unsafe work environment costs you money in claims, in lack of productivity, and in lack of efficiencies. If you have equipment that's damaged and isn't being repaired, then you have equipment that's not running at its maximum efficiency. If employees have to sidestep safety hazards to get their jobs done, that's wasting time too.

There's a hard cost to maintaining a safe environment, but there's a soft cost too. If you have an unsafe workplace, word gets around. You're going to have a hard time recruiting and retaining employees. They might come to you for a time, but no one wants to put themselves in harm's way. Conversely, everyone also knows when a company is safe, and they want to work there. Be that company.

 **CHAPTER 13**

Evaluations and Reviews

How do you know when it's time to give someone a promotion? How can you be sure someone's stopped growing in their current position and needs a change? How can you confirm that an employee has reached the critical moment where he or she needs to be terminated? The answer to all these questions is *evaluations*.

Just like you evaluate business (perhaps on a monthly basis when you're looking at your financials), so should you evaluate your staff members. They need to know where they stand. They need to know how they're doing, and so do you.

With proper evaluations, you'll be able to catch problems and nip them in the bud, tweak behaviors before they grow to be habits, and encourage a unified company culture. With steady feedback to your employees and clear goals for where to go next and how to grow, all of your business reviews or evaluations can be positive or at least productive.

Imagine trying to run your business and only looking at your profit and loss statement once a year—most business owners and CEOs couldn't conceive of that. Now, apply that logic to how you give feedback to your employees. It's no different.

You wouldn't dream of driving your car for four years without a tune-up, and humans are much more complicated than cars. Long-running Broadway shows deal with this basic entropy by bringing in the director or associate director now and again to hold rehearsals, keeping the actors on track, tightening the dance numbers, and making sure the production retains that opening-night feel. As the directors of the productions that are our businesses, we also need to provide that clarity and alignment.

HR INSIDER TIP: ANNUAL FORMAL REVIEW AND SALARY RAISES

It's time to break the formal annual review and the yearly raise apart from each other. The review should only be a performance evaluation; it shouldn't be a compensation review. You should do everything in your power to separate those two discussions. When it's time to do a salary review, do a salary review. You should absolutely consider performance in the salary review, but there are other things you need to consider: What's the latest cost-of-living increase? What money do you have available for merit-based increases? What money do you have available for raises in general? What's the going rate for this position? All these things should be considered in two separate sessions.

How and when you review/evaluate your employees is a matter of personal choice. Evaluations take time. It takes time to sit down and discuss, asking, "What concerns do you have? Here's what I've seen. Have you thought about this?"

Ultimately, the more often you meet with your employees throughout the year, the easier the annual formal review becomes. And a very important note here: the items discussed on that annual review should absolutely never be a surprise to your employees.

While monthly reviews are challenging to maintain, monthly check-ins are not. They can be as formal or informal as you want. It's easy to walk the floor and be present, talking to employees, asking how things are going, making mental notes, and keeping track of the general feel of things. This is also a good time to touch base about any safety or time-saving measures and efficiencies your employees may have noticed and to ask what ideas they have or what could be done differently.

In my experience, monthly meetings let me know exactly where my employees are on their goals for the year. Monthly meetings help them understand me better, too. Being an HR person myself, I can get frustrated that my HR manager doesn't do things exactly the same way I do. But by having these points of contact, I can better understand and appreciate her methodology and approach. We can work as a team, each drawing from the other's experience and expertise.

If you can't have a five-minute chat with each employee each month, then work out a system where you see everyone on a quarterly basis.

There are two schools of thought on when to do formal evaluations: one uses the employee's hiring anniversary date, and the other chooses a single time for all the evaluations. My preference is to use the employee anniversary date. Since not all employees are hired at the same time, their evaluation dates are spread throughout the year—maybe two in one month, none the next, etc.

A benefit to doing evaluations once a year is that you know, come December, it's time to do performance evaluations. If you have a large staff, though, you end up with too many evaluations at the same time. This can lead to less thorough evaluations. With this method, you also have to spend a significant amount of time away from your other work. Based on the size of your staff, find a schedule for evaluations that works best for you, the company, and the employees.

Is there a difference between evaluations and reviews? In my opinion, the terms *evaluation* and *review* are virtually interchangeable. You can also think of evaluations as more along the line of the supervisor ranking the employee and of reviews as more of a conversation between the supervisor and employee about where things are at and how things stand. Reviews are a little more "feel good." Evaluations are a little more structured and serious, and they fall into two categories—formal and informal.

Informal evaluations are your monthly meetings, your quarterly meetings, and the desk-side conversations. Informal evaluations are just that: conversations. "How are you doing? How's this going?" But they're also course corrections. "Let's make sure we stay on track. Let's make sure we're both on the same page." They're your clarity-definers. Your formal evaluation is your clarity wrap-up.

I believe formal evaluations should be done at least once a year. You owe it to your employees to sit down once a year, one-on-one, face-to-face, and say, "Here's how you're doing," and to back it up with documentation. You owe it to the business. Again, you don't just look at your profit and loss statement once a year (at least I hope that's not the case), but you definitely look at it once a year when it's tax time.

How specific you get with the formal evaluation is up to you, but it's not unlike an interview. You should have an approach and goals that were planned out in advance.

There are two schools of thought when it comes to formal evaluations: either you have them or you don't. I think you have to have them, even if you hate doing them. I admit, sometimes I hate doing them too, but this year I'm literally practicing what I preach. My HR manager and I have been having monthly meetings (which I implemented with my staff this year), so when we sit down at the formal anniversary review, it should be a no-brainer.

When it comes time to rate the evaluation, it's important that everybody understands what the form is and what the definitions are. I always recommend that you have a well-defined scale. Everyone in the organization should understand what "meets expectations" means, what it looks like, and what it feels like. If you have a solid job description, then you already know what "meets expectations" looks, sounds, and feels like. It's right there in black and white.

When rating, I recommend using a scale of 1–5. When you get into using a scale of 1–10, how do you distinguish between a 6 and 7, or between a 3 and a 4? I usually use a combination of numbers and words. I use the numbers so that I can come up with an overall score, and I use the words to describe the numbers. For example, unsatisfactory, needs improvement, meets expectations, exceeds expectations, and outstanding correlate to 1, 2, 3, 4, and 5, respectively.

Within that scale, I clearly define the difference between "meets expectations" and "exceeds expectations." Everyone should know how someone becomes an "outstanding" or what it means if I give someone an "unsatisfactory." Everyone, including you, should understand the tool before you use the tool.

Someone's evaluation should also consider his or her job description. As you remember, we have essential functions in the job description, and we should be rating, evaluating, and reviewing people based on those same essential functions. In that job description, we also have the soft skills (the competencies). We need to be rating and evaluating people based on those as well—the soft skills go into the fit and culture of the organization and are as important as the essential functions.

THE BENEFITS OF REVIEWS AND EVALUATIONS

The biggest benefit is a sense of clarity for both you and your employees. Perhaps equally important is that you're developing relationships with your employees that are more like adult-adult relationships, rather than adult-child relationships. It reinforces the idea that we're all adults here; this is a business, and it's not personal. And when people are treated like valued adults, they will behave like valued adults.

You're also showing your employees that they have a safety net. They're learning that they may not have met your expectations this month, but through a simple discussion, everyone can move on with a clear path of what to do next and where to go from here.

You'll find that, as you develop a closer, more comfortable relationship with your employees, they'll be more likely to tell you the truth or to bring things up, especially when they know it's safe to do so. Of course, if you're stomping around every month, disrupting things and making people feel like you're spying on them, those monthly check-ins can become pretty stressful. Make sure there is an open exchange of ideas between two adults.

HR INSIDER TIP: PERFECT TIMING

The annual performance review is the perfect time to review and update job descriptions. Job descriptions should not be static; they should be fluid. They should be ever-changing, just like your business is always changing, growing, and morphing. The annual formal review is the best time to make sure the job description truly defines the job and to make changes as necessary.

DOCUMENTING THROUGHOUT THE YEAR

If you don't have a system in place where you're regularly sitting and talking with your employees, I want you to make notes (both positive and negative) throughout the year and put them somewhere safe. This way, when it comes time to sit down and do the annual review, you're not combing through your calendar, trying to remember what happened in the past year or how well the employee performed a certain task six months ago.

The biggest downfall when preparing yearly reviews is that we fail to remember the *whole* year when we sit down to prepare the document. Human nature is to put the most emphasis on recent history. That's not what should inform these reviews. You should not be relying on your emotions or your memory, so write notes and keep track of things (both good and bad). If you do, you'll have everything right at your fingertips when you go to prepare the reviews.

At HR Resolutions, we use an online system to write and store notes. But before that, I just had a computer folder or an actual physical manila folder where I'd store kudos and notes for when things didn't go so well.

SALARY REVIEWS

Most Americans still believe in the Christmas bonus—once a fairly standard thing, it is now basically a thing of the past. Another great American myth is the yearly raise. When it comes to bonuses and pay increases—and you have to keep in mind, I'm writing from my experience as a baby boomer—I was raised to know that my dad got a raise each year. That was the American way. But that's not necessarily the American way anymore.

While I would love to give pay increases every year, I'm not always in a position to do so. In an economy where growth is not always a guarantee, raises and bonuses are very challenging for employers. Instead, I have to look for other ways to increase value.

For example, instead of pay increases one year, we implemented company-provided life insurance, disability insurance, and an employee assistance program. There's a cost to those things, but they also add value. Going back to "total compensation," I make sure that my employees understand the value of what is offered and how that contributes to their bottom line. I'm not secretive about that because I don't want them to say, "Oh, I didn't get a raise this year." I want them to be able to say, "My compensation package changed this year."

There are many other types of rewards that you can offer that don't cost an arm and a leg. It's sometimes just a simple thank-you to an employee, spoken aloud or written in a personal card. At HR Resolutions, our employees know that if we hit a certain revenue level annually, we spend a day at the spa. If someone doesn't want to go to the spa, I give that person the day off. As a spa is not something that's paid directly to the employees, they aren't taxed on it. Frankly, it's a tax write-off for the employer because it's a team-building day and a business expense.

Let's be honest: changing just benefits and not wages doesn't help pay the bills for your employees. From a human perspective, you definitely want to recognize that your employees' costs are increasing just like your costs increase, so you need to be sensitive about making sure that you're paying market rate. That means you want to make sure that you are paying comparably to other companies in your area (rather than just those in the same field of business), because when it comes to jobs, you're recruiting against all the other companies in your area. You want to do what you can to retain your employees. Pay the best you can and be honest with your employees about it.

Find out what's important to your employees. Do they want more education? Do they want to attend a seminar or professional development workshop? A seminar could benefit the work they do for your company, but if you don't pay for it, their only options are skipping it or paying for it out of pocket. It makes sense to add these things to your employees' total compensation packages.

I know of a company that is located above a gym. The CEO got a corporate account at that gym and offered membership to her employees. Not only did this reinforce wellness and provide stress management, it showed that the boss was listening to them when they were talking excitedly about the new (and expensive) gym downstairs.

Professional memberships can be very important to your employees' professional growth and development. They're a good way to be recognized within your industry or profession. Paying for employees' memberships is a type of reward and is part of the total compensation package when you're bringing them on board. While there's a cost to memberships, you're also increasing the value of your employees.

Whichever pay structure you choose, you need to be sure that you're consistent. You need to be sure that you can compete against other businesses and organizations, which means you have to play fair and pay fair.

WHEN AN EMPLOYEE ASKS YOU FOR A RAISE

One of the most awkward work-related meetings is when an employee surprises their employer by asking for a raise, often doing so out of the blue. I usually respond with a version of, "I appreciate you bringing that to my attention. Tell me why you deserve a raise and what you're thinking." (I'd probably respond a little more nicely than that, but if someone wants a raise, I expect that person to tell me, quite frankly, what's in it for me.) I always make the asker do the work. Employees asking for raises need to be able to explain what they've done for me and what they've done for the business. It can't just be a matter of wanting or needing more money. If that was the case, I'd get a raise every day!

Here's an example of a meeting that makes sense: Say my marketing manager asks for a meeting and then shows me that he or she saved the business 30 percent on print ads this year and brought in an additional $20,000 of business through his or her personal trade contacts. Looking at that data, I would say, "You're right. We should look at that." The employee is redefining the position through his or her hard work. I should respond by taking the new situation into consideration and reconsidering the value it has to me.

If, during the meeting, it becomes clear that the employee just wants more money, I typically respond, "I get it. I want more money too. But I can't get more money until we have more sales, so you go get me more business and I'll get you more money. That's how we can work together to make this happen." This takes a potentially negative situation and makes it a proactive plan for change and improvement, and the employee leaves with clear parameters of how to reach that goal. I might also say, "You're in this professional association that we pay for. Are you talking to them? Are you introducing our products and services to them? I'll tell you what. If you can get us three new pieces of business out of that professional association in the next year, we can take a look at a commission or a bonus or any number of things."

Before employees leave this kind of meeting, they should have a clear understanding that they have to contribute to the company and help it to grow before there will be more money to go around.

PERFORMANCE MANAGEMENT

Coaching and counseling are more reasons why it's so important to have conversations with your employees throughout the year. Just the two words themselves conjure up different pictures in your brain. *Coaching* is like mentoring, where we're developing our people and putting training in place to make them better. *Counseling* is a remedy for something that needs to be corrected. The two are still very similar, and we should be looking at any counseling as coaching.

Bottom line, we want our people to do a good job for us. If we have not clarified where employees are letting us down or not meeting expectations, we should be having coaching and mentoring conversations with them. Granted, if I have to have the same coaching conversation a couple of times, I'd better change over to counseling mode. In that case, I'd say, "We're having this conversation again because you are clearly not grasping this."

The first time we had a counseling conversation, I'd fall on my sword and ask whether it's my fault for not explaining it well or being unclear. This is going overboard, but I might say, "I must not have explained myself well. Let me help you understand why it's important to come to work on time. 8:00 a.m. is when our workday begins. Everyone else is here, and you need to be here too. For clarity's sake, our starting time is 8:00 a.m. I'm going to write down that I told you that our starting time is 8:00 a.m., and you can initial that you understood." If they say that they're having trouble waking up, maybe I buy them a little alarm clock. If that doesn't work, I think we have our answer.

Melodrama aside, if we change our mind-set on disciplinary actions to thinking of them as coaching opportunities, we can accomplish much more. Our employees will start to trust us as well, and they'll be more likely to seek us out for coaching and mentoring on their own. They may come to you and say, "I'm having trouble grasping the need for this new policy. Can you help me understand? Can you help me determine my priorities with this change?"

As always, all evaluations come back to clarity, accountability, respect for the employee, and respect for yourself as a business owner. When evaluations are done correctly, everyone moves up the ladder together.

PART 4

Parting Ways

CHAPTER 14

Terminations

This chapter will cover terminations and how best to handle each situation.

When coaching and counseling don't work, it may be time to consider termination. It's okay to say, "You're fired." Sometimes, the reason we don't terminate people is that we're afraid or we don't want to hurt their feelings. You don't want to be the reason that someone loses the means to make money and feed his or her kids. But remember this: if it's not a good fit, then it's best for everyone involved for the misery to come to an end. The longer you let a situation like this go on, the worse things get, the more miserable the individual gets, the more customer problems arise, and the more the cancer spreads to the coworkers.

Don't forget that by not terminating someone, you're also preventing the right person from being able to step into that job. So if you're going to feel bad, why not feel bad about keeping the perfect candidate from earning money at your business?

You have a responsibility to the whole. If you have a bad apple, get it out of the barrel before it spoils the bunch. That happens in apple barrels *and* in organizations. If your good employees constantly see a less-than-stellar employee getting away with everything, they may flip sides and become disgruntled and dissatisfied employees themselves. Why should they be busting their buns when Joe sits in his chair all day listening to music? It won't take long before they decide that they shouldn't.

Let's refer back to the coaching and counseling. One of three things is going to happen when you give somebody a disciplinary notice. One: that person is going to step up, pay attention, and improve. (That's a good thing.) Two: that person is going to give up and resign, removing himself or herself from the situation. (That's also a good thing.) Three: that person is not going to change, and you're going to be able to remove him or her from the situation properly. (This, too, is a good thing.) Only one of those three things is going to happen, but in the end, they're all good things.

HIRE SLOW, FIRE FAST, STEP CAREFULLY, ACT DECISIVELY

When it comes to having the law on your side, keep in mind that there's a difference between having a bad attitude and exhibiting bad behavior. It is difficult to fire someone for being negative. It's annoying, but there may not be any actionable behavior until they start exhibiting that negativity in communications with customers and/or coworkers. That combative communication is the *behavior* associated with the *attitude* of being negative. You're not terminating or disciplining people based on an attitude. You're terminating based on a behavior that has been clearly and thoroughly documented.

Many times, a supervisor will call HR and say, "I am going to fire Tammy today." The HR manager responds, "Okay, where's the documentation?" The supervisor replies that they don't have any, but they've had problems with Tammy for a year. The HR manager replies that Tammy has exceeded the boss's expectations for the last four performance reviews. Here's where you need to choose the risk level you're prepared to take—you can spend time coaching and documenting, or you can cut to the chase.

Unemployment often looks at what the incident that caused the termination was—the straw that broke the camel's back, if you will. What happened?

There are times when it is absolutely appropriate to make an immediate termination, and those things should be crystal clear in your handbook. Obvious grounds for immediate dismissal include theft from the company, coworkers, or customers, sabotage of equipment, threat of bodily harm, and physical violence. For most other things, especially performance-related matters, regulatory and unemployment agencies are going to look for proof of progressive coaching and counseling, as well as for the documented moment when you told that employee, "If you do this again, you will be terminated."

Being able to make that call goes all the way back to the center of the HR wheel—job descriptions—and carries right on through the recruiting and hiring processes. Of course, try as we might, no matter how carefully we prepare our questions and consider our candidates, we all make a bad hire eventually. I don't care how long you've been doing this or what your track record is; it will happen.

As soon as you recognize that you have a bad hire, remember that old adage, "Hire slow, fire fast." Unless you're a masochist, you're going to want to get that person out quickly! And truly, keeping a bad hire around puts you into uncomfortable territory because you're torturing your other employees, your customers, yourself, and even the individual that isn't a fit.

The best thing to do with bad hires is to let them go be productive and happy (or lazy and miserable—it's up to them) somewhere else. Wish them well. Have courage, maintain your dignity, and let them go. And whatever you do, don't lay them off. If you say you're laying them off but turn around and hire for the position next week, you could be facing a lawsuit for your actions. It's best to sever the based on the real, job-related reason.

UNEMPLOYMENT AND REFERENCES

Unemployment is an insurance fund. You've been paying into it, so it's okay to use it. That's what it's there for! But when someone resigns or says that they quit, it's critical to get that voluntary resignation from the person signed, dated, and in writing. Without that record, someone who quit can easily claim that he or she was fired and is entitled to undeserved benefits.

In all honesty, unless you have a lot of terminations, unemployment claims really do not hurt at all. Think of unemployment as a big pie: You're paying into the state's pie fund, as is your employee. Your company is assigned a portion of that pie—X percent of that pie belongs to you and can go to people you've fired. As long as you don't dip into somebody else's piece of the pie, then one claim has very little impact on you. You haven't exceeded what you've paid in.

But if you have a ton of turnover and go outside of your little slice of pie, then in future years you'll be responsible for paying for a larger portion of the pie, as well as paying back the extra pie you "ate" the year before.

While there are unemployment claims that you can avoid, there are a number of situations where unemployment is a completely valid and useful insurance to help and protect your workers.

If you have to cut hours or make a true restructuring where you're moving people around, you may be faced with doing layoffs. When you tell people that they're being laid off, it's almost guaranteed that they're going to get unemployment. As I said, never try to soften the blow of a termination based on performance or conduct by telling someone that they're being laid off. You have less protection against unemployment being claimed, and you fail to sever the tie between you, your company, and your soon-to-be-ex-employee.

If people truly believe that they've been laid off, they may also be expecting you to bring them back at some point. So unless you are truly in a lay-off situation and planning to reintegrate them, it's best to terminate.

When you're in a termination meeting, one of the things that can help is if you talk about unemployment and references. Aside from how they're going to pay their bills, these are two of the things that will be foremost on terminated employees' minds. Help lower their stress and fear by walking them through the process of how it's going to work. Don't make any promises, and let them know that the employer does not decide eligibility for unemployment compensation benefits.

Whether someone is granted unemployment benefits is not your call. I typically explain, "Unemployment is going to send me paperwork. I have a responsibility to complete that paperwork truthfully, but the decision on whether or not you receive unemployment is not mine. The local unemployment bureau decides if you qualify or not."

While it can be frustrating to think that the person who just stole from you for six months might get unemployment benefits, sometimes it's best to just do whatever you can to speed the process along so the trouble goes away, and you can get that person out of your life and out of your company.

When people lose their jobs through no fault of their own, they are generally eligible for unemployment. Here's the really frustrating part, from an employer's standpoint: "through no fault of their own." One would think that coming to work late every day is within a person's control.

One would think that if someone continues to make errors when inputting customer orders, then that would be the person's fault. Not quite—it could be seen as a performance issue. Did you complete process training? Retraining? Counseling? I hope so, because the hearing officer is going to ask the individual, "Did you perform to the best of your abilities?" I guarantee that the person is going to say, "Yes, I did, but their expectations were way too high." Based on that statement, the former employee's failure was outside of his or her control. If the hearing officer agrees, then you're out of luck.

Another common trap is the attendance issue. If a company uses a points system, then on the surface, it seems fair. If you are late, you get so many points. If you're absent, you get so many points, no matter the reason. When you get X number of points, you're terminated. But unemployment is only going to look at the last event. If that last event was the result of an accident on Route 95, that particular instance of tardiness was outside of the individual's control, and they're granted unemployment—even though the other twenty times, they were late because they slept in.

If you don't care whether or not the person gets unemployment, you can simply write, "Employer has no desire to contest," on the unemployment claim form. With that, you're basically telling the bureau, "You make the decision, I'll run with it." In the event that the employee is denied unemployment and he or she appeals, if you don't wish to challenge the application for benefits don't go to the hearing. That way, the hearing officer only gets one side of the story, and since it's the employee's side, the decision is typically reversed.

More problematic than a layoff is a forced resignation. While you might offer someone the opportunity to resign in order to save face (and avoid a lawsuit), it's not uncommon for a supervisor to try to force an employee to resign in order to avoid an unemployment claim. The supervisor may even succeed in bullying or pressuring such people into saying that they resigned, even though they would have been fired if they had stayed. When the unemployment claim comes, the employer responds that the employee resigned. But if the employee is able to demonstrate that they were going to be fired had they not resigned, that will be considered a situation outside of their control, meaning that they qualify for benefits.

As I mentioned before, one thing that helps cool down a termination meeting is to go through the company policy on giving references. Let the person being terminated know that if people call for references, you only share X, Y, and Z. You won't tell callers the reason for the separation or anything else that could keep the person from gainful employment. Remember, you should not generally blacklist anyone, no matter how much you might want to.

When those reference check calls do come in, be careful and truthful. If you can't say something nice, don't say anything at all, or find the one good thing the person did and focus on that. No matter what question they ask you, answer with, "They came to work on time." The caller should pick up on that tactic and read between the lines.

One question you're almost always asked is, "Would you hire so-and-so again?" I wouldn't answer yes or no unless I have the documentation to back up why the person would not be eligible for rehire and a signed release. You could also say, "Our company policy is that if someone is terminated, they're not eligible for rehire. If someone does not give proper notice, they're also not eligible for rehire."

TERMINATIONS AND LEVELS OF VOLATILITY

If you expect that someone is going to take a termination badly, you'll want to consider a few options. Can the termination take place outside of the office? Are you able to do it in the morning, before anyone else comes in? Can it happen after work hours, when people have gone home? In deciding this, you also need to think about protecting yourself.

If you believe that it's going to get violent, there are some definite steps you should take. Sit closest to the door, so your exit path is clear. Have someone outside the office or conference room ready to dial 911. If you are seriously concerned, you may want to have a police officer and/or security guard present. In a volatile situation, you should not have anything nearby that could be used as a weapon; this includes pens, staplers, and paperweights.

If you're in a termination meeting and someone starts yelling and acting the fool, shut them down immediately. If the behavior continues, say, "This meeting is over. You either need to exit the building or I can call the police, because at this point, you're trespassing." Usually, they're yelling because they're angry, and they're angry because they're disappointed, hurt, and scared. Mentioning the police may snap them back to reality. In that case, they'll generally do what you ask.

If they *don't* stop yelling or begin to threaten you, then end the meeting and ask them to leave immediately and call security if you're lucky enough to have that service. It's possible that worse things are going to happen. First of all, you're going to get an unemployment claim, which is fine. You pay into that insurance anyway. Second of all, they may sue you. I say that very nonchalantly, but in all honesty, people can sue you at any time for any reason, and it's certainly better to be sued than to be hit in the head by a big metal stapler.

As a precaution, you may want to explore employment practices liability insurance (EPLI). EPLI is an insurance policy specifically covering many employment practice lawsuits. If sued, you pay a deductible, but the insurance takes care of the defense, fines, penalties, charges, and the settlement. It's well worth the money. I have it, even with only four employees. If you have done your due diligence and you have documented everything, then the only thing you have to be afraid of is the nuisance of the time, effort, and energy it's going to take.

HR INSIDER TIP: NEVER FIRE ON A FRIDAY

This is an old adage from back when people had to physically go into the unemployment office and file. Even though you can now file for unemployment 24/7, I still follow that "never fire on a Friday" rule because you don't want people stewing for two days before they can walk into the unemployment office or attorney's office. If you fire people on a Friday, all they can do is sit around and drink vodka and kvetch with their friends for two days, getting themselves all riled up. It's better to fire people early in the week so they can calmly get things in order.

We had a termination that took place after an individual threatened the company in front of a vendor, saying he was going to come back and shoot up the whole place. We take threats very seriously, so when we went to terminate that individual, there were no write-ups leading up to that incident. His threat was grounds for immediate termination.

Because the employee worked in a shop with heavy equipment and tools that could be used as weapons, we actually called the police to be present during the termination. As we approached, I had the manager remove his tie because that can also be used as a weapon.

When we arrived, we called him outside of the shop where we were waiting with police in the background. The employee walked out of the shop with a tool in his hand—something with a weird little hook on it. Playing dumb, I said, "Oh, that's an interesting little tool. Can I see that for a minute? What's it do?" He handed it over to me, and I put it behind my back so that I could drop it if I needed to, in case he went for me.

We took those precautions to protect ourselves, our coworkers, and the employee himself. Afterward, we also put the facility on an immediate lockdown for forty-eight hours for a kind of cooling-off period and had the police make extra patrols through the area. In most cases, terminated employees are angry, sad, and scared—even raging and out of control—but they generally cool down within a couple of days and begin to move on.

It's very, very rare that a former employee will come back for physical retribution. However, the possibility is there—you've seen it on the news—but how *often* do you see it on the news, compared to how many employers are out there in the United States, hiring and firing people on a daily basis? That tells me that it rarely happens and that the chances of having it happen to me are very, very, very slim.

BEYOND COMMON SENSE: PROTECTIVE MEASURES AND PROPER FILES

I always recommend that you keep former employees' personnel files through your open tax year, but check your federal and state regulations for rules on record retention. There are statutes of limitations on when you can be sued through the regulatory agencies. The maximum is generally two years, so you want to keep files for at least that long.

If you catch wind that somebody is considering suing you, lock down everything. Keep it all—that includes electronic communications, which can be obtained through what's called e-discovery.

Even the meekest employees can turn on you once you've let them go. They may stuff a couple of pens in their bag to show you who's boss, or they may clear the entire contact database on their computer and delete all the marketing files.

If you know that you're going to let someone go, you'll want to have a plan that's set and ready to go with whomever handles your IT. For example, my IT is outsourced, so as I head into the meeting, I'll send a text, "Meeting now." Because I've told them ahead of time that this was going to be happening, they know it's time to change the passwords on that employee's e-mails and disable remote access.

After terminating people, do not let them go back to their desk or computer. And because most work e-mails can be accessed from smartphones now, IT should already have changed their password.

The person who has just been terminated should not be left alone in your environment, but you also have to be cautious of a civil suit for intentional infliction of emotional distress. I guarantee that anytime I've walked somebody to his or her desk and hovered, the rest of the office knows that person has been fired. You have to be as discreet as you can be while still protecting the company. Still, when I take people to their desks to clean out their personal things, I have a duty to make sure that it's only their personal things they're taking.

An alternative is to say, "We need you to leave the building now, but would you like to come back tonight after hours to get your things? Or I can meet you here tomorrow, before the building opens." If that's not a viable option, say, "We will pack up your personal belongings and ship them to you."

Terminated employees often ask, "What about my personal contacts and e-mail?" Your response should be, "We will go through your contacts and send you those that are obviously not company-related." If they ask to get them now and say that they don't trust you, you answer, "I'm sorry, your computer is company property." Remember, no good deed goes unpunished, so don't get sucked in.

What you *should* do is make sure that any documentation you need to give the employee has been prepared ahead of time. Make sure that you're prepared when you go into termination meetings. You should know what you're going to say, what you need to tell them, and what you need to get from them, including any passwords, keys, credit cards, and technology. Be in control of the situation from the first moment. Be prepared to have their technology cut off while you're in the meeting. Know exactly who is going to execute what steps. Know where their e-mails are going to go and where their phone calls are going to be directed. The more you have in place, the better prepared you'll be for the unexpected.

When it comes to sharing the news of the departure with your other employees, again, prepare what you're going to say ahead of time. In my experience, less is better. It's perfectly reasonable to say, "So-and-so is no longer with the company." End of story. Some may choose to reach out to the former employee to get the scoop, but most won't. Either way, it's not your problem.

Terminating an employee is one of the most stressful situations you'll have at work, but with good planning and documentation in place and an exit strategy ready to go, you'll be ahead of the curve.

CHAPTER 15

Resignations

There are two kinds of reasons for a person to leave a company: involuntary reasons (termination, restructuring, and layoffs) and voluntary reasons (resignations and retirements).

Whenever employees voluntarily leave the company—even with resignations and retirements—you want to get it in writing. If they will not give you anything in writing or if it just doesn't make sense for them to do so, then send them a letter stating, "We accept your voluntary resignation, given to so-and-so on such-and-such date, effective on such-and-such date." You want that documentation in the event that they file for unemployment in the future.

Here's an example of what that might look like. An employee leaves your company to go to another job. That person's new job doesn't work out, however, so he or she has been fired and is now eligible for unemployment. However, that person didn't work with the new company long enough to have a stake in that company's slice of the unemployment pie. So where is unemployment going to look to? *Your* slice of the pie. Except, since you have that signed document saying that the person in question left voluntarily, that person can't access your pie. This is called "relief from charges." You want written resignation so that you can request this "relief" now and in the future.

And then there are those crazy days when somebody just yells, "I quit, I quit, I quit," and storms out. You can follow that dramatic episode with a letter saying, "We accept your voluntary resignation given in the break room on June 9th." The person may come back saying that he or she didn't mean it, but with that letter in hand, you can apologize by saying, "I'm sorry, but you said it, you meant it, and we have already accepted."

HR INSIDER TIP: UNUSED VACATION

Some states require that earned, unused vacation should be paid no matter what, even if someone quits or is fired. Be sure you know what your state wage guidelines are.

Make sure that your company policy doesn't require a notice period. You may be in an *at-will* state, which means you can terminate an employee at will and your employees can leave employment at will, with or without notice

You can request notice, but if you *require* it, then you may be required to give it too, possibly giving up your at-will status—believe me, you don't want to do that. You want the right to let someone go on the spot, if necessary. Most employees will give you at least a two-week notice as a matter of courtesy, but don't expect it unless you are prepared to give your employees notice in every situation.

There are instances where employees will wait until the very last Friday before they start their new jobs to tell you that they're not coming back. You may want to think about why they do this. Were they worried about retribution? Did they feel so uncomfortable talking to you that they didn't want to deal with a possible confrontation? Do they simply hate working for you? Whatever the reason, they're gone now. Make whatever adjustments you need to and move on. (And as an aside, if a new employee is coming to work for you without giving notice to his or her last boss, take note. That person may end up doing the same thing to you when he or she is ready to move on!)

As employers, we have the right to accept employees' resignations, effective immediately. We don't have to accept the terms of their notice, and we don't have to pay them for any more days past the day they resign (unless we let them keep working, obviously). If someone gives you two months' notice, it's your right to say, "That's okay, we choose to terminate you today."

If you go that route, however, keep in mind that you do have some exposure to unemployment claims for the time between the day you terminate such employees and the date they offered as their last when they gave notice. Using that formula, if they give two weeks' notice and you say, "You can go today," then you have effectively removed them from work for two weeks. After their two-week notice period is over, they would no longer be eligible for unemployment. Two weeks of unemployment may be worth getting these employees out the door, especially considering that there's always a one-week waiting period with unemployment. Don't offer to pay someone through his or her notice period as an incentive not to take unemployment. People can take your pay *and* receive unemployment benefits, so unless you want them to get one week of unemployment plus the two weeks of salary that you're paying them to sit at home, do nothing!

The other possibility is if you say, "You may leave today," and the employee calls the new employer, who agrees to start the employee the next day. In this case, you have no unemployment exposure at all.

THINGS TO KNOW BEFORE THEY GO

For any kind of exit from the organization, you need to check your state regulations regarding when the final payment is due. Sometimes, you are required to present exiting employees with their final pay at the exit interview. There are only a few states that require this, but be sure you know if you are in one of those states.

You should conduct an exit interview whenever you are able. The purpose of an exit interview is to find out what you're doing right and what you can do better. There are some things you can't change—you can only pay what you can pay—but if people are leaving because they think the office environment is stifling or because their ideas are always shot down, you can immediately start to address those issues with the employees you still have.

When possible, have someone neutral conduct the exit interview. It should never, ever, *ever* be conducted by the supervisor. I've started doing exit interviews online, so consider this an unpaid plug for SurveyMonkey. What's great about an online survey is that you can send it to employees after they've gone (and after they've had time to distance themselves a little). It's important to find out why someone has left—why they *really* left.

Don't just collect your exit interviews and file them away. Collect and analyze the data—another reason something like SurveyMonkey is so great. Depending on what version you have, it can analyze the data for you.

The reason you're doing an exit interview is to find out what you're doing right and what you can do better. Let your employees give you a little clarity on their way out the door, as a final parting gift.

 **CHAPTER 16**

After They've Gone

Your former employees may be out of sight, but they shouldn't be out of mind. They're part of the institutional history of your organization forever.

On the positive side, if employees left of their own accord but had a positive experience with your company, you may find yourself working with them again in a freelance or consulting capacity. At the very least, they'll be a great brand ambassador for you. If and when possible, maintain a positive relationship going forward.

If employees resign and move on professionally, they may be a perfect fit for you again in the future. Sometimes the best new hire is someone who's already worked for you—think of the time you would save in onboarding alone! If the right position becomes available, consider former employees who have left amicably. Former employees already have a relationship with you and may have maintained bonds with other employees, customers, and clients; they have existing knowledge of the company and the company culture, and, while out in the world working for other people, they will have gained new skills and ideas that they can now bring back to share with you, enriching your company's depth of knowledge and experience and even growing your list of contacts and possible clients.

LET GO WITH GRACE, BUT COVER YOUR BASES

It's human nature for you to take it personally when employees resign, but don't. Wish them well. Throw them a going-away luncheon and congratulate them when you announce it to the rest of the company. "Hey, George is pursuing other opportunities. We appreciate everything that he did for us while he was here, and we wish him well in the future."

Letting someone go with grace sends the message to your remaining employees that you care about them and their happiness. You want to be a good employer, but no job is a fit for everybody. And there isn't always an opportunity for someone to rise up through the ranks of a company. Don't forget that your employees are on their own journeys, too.

Following a termination, resignation, or retirement, you want to make sure that you've retrieved all company property. I recommend getting it all at once—keys, credit cards, badges—anything and everything you can think of, so you don't have to keep going after ex-employees for things. Less contact is better when it comes to terminated employees.

If there is any risk of volatility, instability, retribution, or retaliation from ex-employees, consider the relatively inexpensive cost of changing all the locks and issuing new keys to the cost of having to buy all new computers after they come back and smash things to pieces. Protecting yourself, your business, and your current employees is definitely worth the cost

In the case of a company credit card, you can always call the credit card company and cancel an ex-employee's card (or the whole account, if you have to). You may want to do this, considering how easy it is to store information and buy things without needing an actual card in hand.

It's impossible to keep your staff from continuing their friendships with former coworkers, so don't even try. Whether someone resigned, retired, or was fired, chances are they still have relationships with people on your staff and are often connected through social media.

Sometimes, a former employee will use friends still on staff to dig for information, even if it's just a way to remain connected. Remind employees that, while they may still be friends, that person is no longer an employee and that information related to the internal workings of the company are no longer his or her business. Legally, you can give your employees guidelines, but nothing is actually enforceable unless you have a confidentiality agreement of some sort or the information is protected under law.

In the case of an involuntary termination, there is absolutely nothing wrong with telling your employees, "If so-and-so reaches out to you, please let us know." You should also remind them that if the former employee's contact makes them at all uncomfortable, they should let you know right away so you can help.

I discourage current employees from initiating contact with former employees, but it's going to happen—they want to make sure that their friend is all right. Again, you can give guidelines to help keep things professional; just be careful that you're not propping open a door to a vindictive or volatile ex-employee.

HR INSIDER TIP: BOARD MEMBERS ON SITE

Like a beloved former employee, sometimes board members feel as though they have unlimited access to the workplace. But when board members come to visit, they are still visitors. They need to sign in, they need to be escorted, and sometimes, they need to be managed. It's harder to have that kind of conversation with a board member than with a retiree, since you probably don't want to make waves, but board members stand to profit when the company is running smoothly and efficiently, with limited disruptions. If there's an issue with constant or lengthy visits, you need to deal with it.

The hardest thing for any organization is to remember that when a former employee comes back to visit, they're a visitor. If your visitors have to be escorted around your building, then your former employee has to be escorted. It's hard to enforce because old habits kick in, but it's truly a protective measure for both you and that former employee. Consider if your retirees are coming back to chat five minutes with this person and five minutes with that person, they can effectively take hours away from the collective workday. My suggestion is that you manage those visits. Invite them back for lunch on a Friday or have them join the staff for a get-together after work.

It can be especially difficult for retirees to make the break from your company. They may have been working and socializing with these same people for twenty, thirty, or even forty years. Sitting at home, they might not know what to do with themselves. Be gracious, but be firm. Let them know you're glad to see them, then be sure to show them the appropriate way to move forward.

People may move on from the company, but we still need to respect that they were an employee of ours and played a part in our organization. We also have to respect their privacy, their dignity, and their future. They have a right to go and try to make a living. As long as you manage those relationships with respect, you'll be fine.

CONCLUSION

Failure to Plan Is Planning to Fail

The best HR management comes from making a plan, however simple, then conveying it clearly to your staff and sticking to it. The best HR managers—accidental or otherwise—actively listen to their employees, engage in interactive dialogues to solve problems, and work steadily and swiftly to ensure and maintain a safe work environment.

Employees who work under a top-notch "accidental HR manager" are crystal clear on their job descriptions and how their positions relate to the success of the company. They understand and connect to the mission, vision, and values of the company, and they treat coworkers with respect.

We keep returning to a few key themes in this book: clarity, respect, honesty, and the need to *document, document, document.* Let those four themes guide you as you begin to implement these best practices at your own company. While your employees might bristle at the first changes, those four themes will help you to bring everyone on board.

Don't feel the need to implement everything in this book all at once. Rushing into things headfirst will only create more problems. Instead, plan to implement one section of this book at a time.

Clarity

If there is only one thing that you can do, I recommend that you start by getting your job descriptions in order. They are truly the hub of the wheel, and everything else stems from those job descriptions. Even if that's the *only* thing you do, it will have an immediate impact and will start to affect every other aspect of your organization in a positive way. You, as the owner or manager, will have a better understanding of how everything fits together and flows, just from implementing that one section. Your employees will feel that shift, too. Make sure your employees understand their job descriptions, and watch the subtle changes that begin to take place in the company culture.

Respect

The other thing to do right away is to implement the Golden Rule—treating people the way that you would like to be treated. As cliché as this sounds, it provides clear goals and guidelines, such as speaking in a respectful tone, thanking others for their contributions, calmly coaching and mentoring when things go wrong, giving others the benefit of the doubt, and listening to suggestions and concerns.

Honesty

This is where you walk the walk. Create the environment that *you* would love to work in. If you were an employee, would you want to work at your company? If the answer isn't *yes*, then go back to your mission, vision, and values, and start there. Bring yourself into alignment with your own expectations: that's the best way to be an honest leader. Create the kind of company where you would thrive as an employee, and then find others who will thrive in that environment. It's okay if that's not everybody, and it's okay if current staff members choose to move on as you get your house in order.

Document, Document, Document

Get in the habit of keeping notes, tracking changes, and collecting data. You can start documenting today, even before you put together your job descriptions. Pull up your calendar right now and make a note: "Decided to rewrite job descriptions and start documenting good and bad incidents at work." Figure out a system, however simple, and get started. It doesn't have to be fancy to be functional.

Think about what you would like your company to be remembered for, beyond the products you sell and the services you provide. Are you here to provide a quality work environment where your employees can thrive as individuals while working on a team? Do you want your employees to have a healthy work-life balance? Do you want your employees to be proud to work for you and your company? Do you want your company to be known for the good work it does in the community or for the educational opportunities it provides for your staff members and their families?

Figure out what matters most to you. Share your excitement and passion with your staff. Find out what matters to them. See if you're in alignment. Let that knowledge influence how you walk forward into the future, together: a united team with an exceptional leader.

Not everybody believes that HR is fun, but it's always been one of my company's core values. We believe it. We are passionate about it. We love it. We breathe it. If someone doesn't get that, he or she is not going to be successful at HR Resolutions. We may not be curing cancer, but HR is still serious stuff—it's where you clarify your business ethics and set them down in print. It's the heart and soul of your values that keep your company moving forward with employees that are whole and healthy, happy and productive, and free of the drama that bogs so many companies down.

Ben Franklin said, "If you fail to plan, you are planning to fail." You may have accidentally ended up in HR, but you no longer have to bumble along, causing more distractions and putting your business and employees at risk—far from it.

You now have more than the basic requirements for moving forward in HR—in fact, you have the makings of a master's degree in HR with a good grasp of best practices. Having clarity on your HR role is going to set you apart from your competitors. Frankly, that's what this is all about—finding a way to set yourself apart so you can draw the best candidates who will make the best employees, do the best work, and help your company grow.

In my world of HR, there is nothing better than hearing the joy in employees' voices when you offer them a job that they really want. That joy continues as they flourish in a position that is a perfect fit for them and for your company. That joy can continue, even as they make a change and move on, because you know exactly what you're going to do to bring in the next candidate for that position so that you and your company can continue to shine.

 **ABOUT HR RESOLUTIONS**

OUR MISSION

We work side by side with our client partners helping them create workplaces where employees WANT to come to work—every day!

OUR CORE VALUES

Going the extra mile for our clients is second nature to us.

ALWAYS do right—no matter what.

Paying our "community rent" isn't considered work.

HR is FUN!

We "get it" (things aren't always black and white; our clients do have a business to run).